THE BATTLE OF BRITAIN

By the same Author

1 (overleaf) *Messerschmitt 110 long-range fighters over a south-coast town*

THE BATTLE
OF
BRITAIN

BASIL COLLIER

LONDON
B. T. BATSFORD LTD

First published 1962

© BASIL COLLIER, 1962

MADE AND PRINTED IN GREAT BRITAIN BY
WILLIAM CLOWES AND SONS LTD, LONDON AND BECCLES
FOR THE PUBLISHERS
B. T. BATSFORD LTD
4 FITZHARDINGE STREET, PORTMAN SQUARE, LONDON W.1

To Three Men

HUGH, LORD DOWDING
who laid the foundations and whose foresight and firmness
preserved the fighter force from disintegration
even before the battle started

SIR KEITH PARK
whose tactical skill and insight passed the crucial test

MAX, LORD BEAVERBROOK
under whose guidance
more Hurricanes and Spitfires were produced
than once seemed possible

CONTENTS

LIST OF ILLUSTRATIONS

LIST OF ILLUSTRATIONS

LIST OF ILLUSTRATIONS

ACKNOWLEDGMENT

The Author and Publishers wish to thank the following for permission to reproduce the illustrations which appear in this book:

Air Vice-Marshal Sir Quintin Brand, K.B.E., D.S.O., M.C., D.F.C. for fig. 22

Central Press Photos Ltd for fig. 29

The Editor of *Flight* for fig. 27

Fox Photos Ltd for figs. 26 and 44

The Imperial War Museum for figs. 3, 11, 12, 19-21, 23-25, 35-37, 46 and 47

Keystone Press Agency Ltd for figs. 14 and 40

Lafayette Ltd for fig. 13

Planet News for fig. 15

The *Radio Times* Hulton Picture Library for figs. 10, 16, 39 and 41

The Sport and General Press Agency Ltd for fig. 2

Süddeutsche Verlag, Munich, for figs. 4-9, 30-32, 43 and 45

Verlag Ullstein, Berlin, for figs. 1, 28, 33, 34, 38 and 42

I

Introduction

ONE OF THE surprises of the Second World War was the comparatively poor use made by the belligerents of air power, especially in
the early stages but also later. In spite of the wide publicity given
before the war to hopes and fears that air power might become a
decisive weapon, neither Britain nor Germany provided herself by
1939 with an air force adequate or suitable in all respects for the
tasks that lay ahead.

This omission was all the more remarkable on the British side,
for only a few years had elapsed since the Government then in
office deliberately chose to stake the country's future on a strong
air force. To understand where British policy went astray, it is
necessary to go back to the beginnings of rearmament in 1933.

In November of that year the leaders of the all-party National
Government, who had come to office on a platform of retrenchment
and collective security within the League of Nations, were forced
by the imminent breakdown of the League to appoint a committee
of experts for the purpose of advising them how to plug the worst
gaps in the national defences. The committee, known as the Defence
Requirements Committee, was a very strong one. It was headed by
Sir Maurice Hankey, Secretary to the Cabinet and a mine of information on defence matters. Its members included the Chiefs of Staff
of the three fighting services, the Secretary to the Treasury and the
Permanent Under-Secretary of State for Foreign Affairs. In other
words, the committee comprised the three service chiefs and the
three leading civil servants.

In February, 1934, the Defence Requirements Committee reported
that the most urgent need was to lay the foundations of an Expeditionary Force which could, in case of need, be sent to the Low
Countries, not only as a means of preserving the traditional balance
of power in Europe but also as a means of keeping a hostile bomber

force at arm's length. At the same time they recommended that an existing scheme of air defence at home should be completed as a matter of 'first importance', and that something should be done to bring the country's notoriously old-fashioned coast defences up to date. They added that, notwithstanding the obvious danger of war in the Far East, where Japan was already deeply embroiled in China, the 'ultimate potential enemy' was Germany, who might be ready for war by 1938 or 1939.

Unwilling to ask the taxpayer for the seventy-one million pounds which these measures would have cost, the leaders of the National Government dished themselves in the eyes of posterity by rejecting the opinion of the very men whom they had appointed to advise them. They decided not to prepare an Expeditionary Force, but to concentrate on the air force in the hope that expansion of the home-based bomber force might induce the Germans to think twice before attacking France or Britain. The Chiefs of Staff incurred a heavy responsibility for what followed by not pressing their dissent to the point of resignation. The civil servants, on the other hand, can be acquitted, since they were not free to resign and had no means of exerting pressure on the Government.

The policy of the bomber deterrent failed utterly to deflect Hitler from his purpose. Ultimately a Conservative Government led by Neville Chamberlain was forced, after all, to form an Expeditionary Force and send it to the Continent when war broke out. But Chamberlain, who had refused as Chancellor of the Exchequer in the National Government to find the money for a balanced strategy, continued as Prime Minister to hope that an expanded bomber force would prove a cheap means of persuading Hitler to see reason. He was sustained in his error by the absurdly inflated claims made for the bomber arm by many airmen.

In spite of the glaring weaknesses of Britain's military policy from 1934 until after Munich, that policy might at least have been expected to result in the creation of a strong bomber force, since that was what the statesmen said they wanted. As things turned out, the country was denied even that advantage. On the outbreak of war the British bomber force was deficient in first-line strength and depth, its equipment was largely obsolescent, and its crews could not reach well-defended objectives in daylight, or find them after dark without new devices which were not perfected until the later stages of the war. Even when those deficiencies were made good, the taxpayer gained only a moderate benefit from his involuntary investment in mass destruction, for the force was largely misused in pursuit of the will o' the wisp of a so-called 'strategic bombing' programme directed to no clearly-defined or practically-attainable end. Meanwhile the situation in 1939 and 1940 was that preparation of the Expeditionary Force had been deferred until the eleventh hour, and that only perfunctory attempts had been made to give it the air support it needed.

The one redeeming feature of Britain's ill-starred attempt to match Germany's air expansion was that, as the outcome of plans laid as early as the 1920s and recast in 1934 and later years, the country did begin the war with at least the nucleus of a sound system of air defence. That proponents of strategic bombing did not succeed in starving the system of aircraft for the benefit of the bomber force was due largely to the intervention of Sir Kingsley Wood, who succeeded Lord Swinton as Secretary of State for Air in May, 1938. On the advice of Sir Thomas Inskip, Minister for Co-ordination of Defence, Kingsley Wood insisted in the autumn of that year that the fighter force should have first claim on the aircraft industry.

Swinton himself deserves to be remembered for the part he played in giving the system the early-warning radar (at first called R.D.F.) which made possible the interception of fast-moving modern bombers. He shares the credit with R. A. (afterwards Sir Robert) Watson-Watt, the begetter of the project; with H. T. (afterwards Sir Henry) Tizard, its chief scientific backer; and with Air Chief Marshal Sir Hugh (afterwards Lord) Dowding, who was Air Member for Research and Development when radar was adopted, and who became his own best customer when he assumed control of the air defences a year later.

On the German side, the leaders of the revived Luftwaffe long shared the view that so-called 'strategic' bombing could play a decisive part—an idea never abandoned by the British Air Staff or entirely relinquished by Herman Göring, the first-war fighter ace who doubled the roles of political head of the German Air Ministry and nominal Commander-in-Chief of the Luftwaffe. The German Air Staff changed their minds as a result of experience gained in the Spanish Civil War, and came to the conclusion that the proper function of an air force was to pave the way for an advancing army. This was a step in the right direction; but the Germans went too far by making their air force too exclusively an instrument of tactical support. The Luftwaffe scored spectacular successes in the Scandinavian campaign, and again in France and the Low Countries, where it worked in close co-operation with the other services and took its orders largely from commanders of land forces whom it helped to keep in touch with an ever-changing tactical situation. When the time came for it to undertake more methodical operations on lines which could not be successfully improvised from day to day, the German system did not work so well. Preparing for a landing in Britain was a task involving the strategic application of air power, not in the loose sense in which airmen talked of 'strategic bombing', but in the sense which distinguishes between strategy and tactics. Out of their depth where the need was not for brilliant improvisation but for forethought and determination, the German leaders threw away the advantage of initial numerical superiority and failed dismally to rise to the occasion.

Since war is essentially a clash of wills, the personalities of commanders are always important. In Sir Hugh Dowding the British air defences had, from 1936 until the battle was over, a chief whose practical experience as an air commander went back to the Somme, and whose character and seniority enabled him to take a strong line in his frequent clashes with authority. In his own service he had the reputation of being stubborn. If to know that one is right where many of one's contemporaries are wrong is to be stubborn, the reproach was just. A few years before the outbreak of war, Dowding was passed over for the post of Chief of the Air Staff, possibly because he had never thought the bomber invincible and was therefore reckoned too defensively-minded. To this lucky stroke of fate the country owed command of the air defences, at the crucial time in 1940, by the one officer of first-rate ability, and character to match, whom the new profession of airman had brought to the fore in any air force.

The German air formations which attacked Britain in the summer of 1940 had no leaders of Dowding's calibre. Field-Marshals Kesselring and Sperrle, commanding the air fleets principally concerned, were able and experienced officers; but they were not an effective counterweight to the swashbuckling Göring, whose failure

2 *Reich Marshal Herman Göring*

THE RIVAL COMMANDERS

3 *Air Chief Marshal Sir Hugh Dowding*

4 *German Council of War, September 5, 1940. Behind Hitler is General Jodl, and on his left stand Field-Marshal Brauchitsch and Grand-Admiral Raeder*

to formulate clear strategic aims, and stick to them, was a major factor in Germany's defeat.

The chief tactical role on the British side was played by Air Vice-Marshal K. R. Park (afterwards Air Chief Marshal Sir Keith Park), commanding the air defences of south-eastern England under Dowding. Not naturally a cautious man, Park showed the instinct of a born tactician by refusing to commit his whole force until he was in a position to deliver a crushing blow at an enemy worn out by a series of vain attempts to bring him to premature action. Men are seldom conscious of all the motives that shape their actions at moments of supreme crisis, and Park would probably have denied in the early stages of the battle that he was holding back. The fact remains that he handled his force with superb restraint until the moment came for a decisive stroke. His achievement was all the more praiseworthy since he was subjected to a good deal of pressure from critics who urged him to commit his whole strength prematurely.

It has been said that, in military matters, legend usually has ten years' start over truth. Legend is not necessarily myth. There is nothing mythical about the skill and courage of the young fighter pilots who gained an undying reputation as 'the few'. At the same time, it is important to understand that the Battle of Britain was not won by isolated acts of heroism. When the struggle began in the summer of 1940, Dowding and his staff had been preparing for it for four years; Göring and his subordinate commanders were mentally and morally unready for the task that faced them in consequence of their swift success in France and of Hitler's decision to prepare for a landing in Britain. Their plans were made in haste, their strategy and tactics not well pondered. In spite of the German reputation for thoroughness, and the British reputation for muddling through, Fighter Command's victory was the triumph of foresight and organisation over improvisation and muddled thinking.

Like the British and Americans four years later, the Germans faced in 1940 the problem of putting troops ashore on a hostile coast. In the German case the difficulty of the undertaking was enormously increased by the overwhelming superiority of the Royal Navy in surface craft. This factor made it impossible for the Germans to contemplate a landing without undisputed air superiority.

Given air superiority they might be able—although even then it was not certain that they would be able—to prevent the Royal Navy from sinking their troop-transports, barges and supply ships.

The story of the Battle of Britain is therefore the story of Göring's attempt, and failure, to gain air superiority over England and the English Channel as an indispensable prelude to invasion. With habitual over-confidence, Göring hoped that his victory in the air would be so complete that only a token landing would be necessary. The fact remains that establishment of the right conditions for a landing was the be-all and end-all of the German effort.

At this stage it should be pointed out that, although it has become customary to regard the Battle of Britain as having begun in the summer of 1940 and continued until the autumn, the whole series of engagements which took place during that period cannot really be called a battle as the term is generally understood by military historians. From a strictly military point of view it would be better to regard these engagements as a series of skirmishes leading up to two decisive actions on September 15. This definition has the advantage of bringing the Battle of Britain into line with the other decisive battles of history, which were predominantly one-day affairs, but is obviously too much out of step with established usage to be generally adopted. At the same time it is worth bearing in mind when the tactical and strategic lessons of the fighting are considered.

Göring began his attempt early in July with a limited offensive designed to establish local superiority over the Straits of Dover, temporarily close the Straits to British shipping in daylight, test Dowding's strength and induce him to wear out his forces prematurely. Dowding, who had fought tenaciously to preserve his command from disintegration during the Battle of France, responded with a caution which brought him, not for the first or last time, into conflict with the Air Staff. Although the Air Staff do not seem to have shown much understanding of Dowding's problems, it is only fair to point out that they were under constant pressure from the Admiralty, who were much concerned at the threat to merchant shipping and destroyers in the Straits.

Towards the middle of August Göring opened his main offensive. His primary object was to smash the Royal Air Force, both by destroying aerodromes and other objectives on the ground, and by bringing about a series of major fighter actions on terms unfavourable to his opponents. Always eager to do too much, he hoped also to continue the offensive against shipping, weaken British anti-invasion forces, and stage so impressive a demonstration of his power that the British Government and people would become convinced of the uselessness of carrying on the struggle.

On the first day Park inflicted heavy losses on inadequately-escorted German bomber formations without committing more than a small part of his force. Air Vice-Marshal Sir Quintin Brand, on Park's right, also fought successful actions. Göring responded by ordering his subordinate commanders, Kesselring and Sperrle, to devote more of their fighters to close escort. The ultimate result was to reduce the effectiveness of the German fighter force and thus diminish Kesselring's chance of winning an all-out fighter battle if and when he persuaded Park to fight one.

In obedience to orders given by Göring before the offensive began, on the second day of heavy fighting General Stumpff, commanding the air forces in Denmark and Norway, sent his bombers, some weakly escorted and some unescorted, across the North Sea to attack objectives in Northumberland and Yorkshire. This led to a series of engagements which were tactically decisive, inasmuch as Stumpff lost a sixth of his force and was henceforth relegated to a minor role. An interesting feature of the day's events was the bold step taken by Air Vice-Marshal R. E. Saul, commanding the air defences north of the Derwent, in sending a squadron of Hurricanes more than eighty miles from their base on the Firth of Forth to fight near Newcastle.

After further unsuccessful attempts to bludgeon his way to a decision on August 16 and 18, Göring saw that he had made the mistake of not beginning by concentrating specifically on destruction of the British fighter force. When major attacks were resumed on August 24 after a period of indifferent weather, the chief role was assigned to Kesselring, who tried everything he knew to bring Park to a clinch. A series of smashing blows at his sector aerodromes put Park in a perilous position, but he resisted the temptation to fight a losing battle on his opponent's terms, and preserved his force substantially intact through a week of crisis. The essence of his tactics continued to be to engage the enemy's bombers as often as he could, and his fighters only when he must.

Unable to wait longer, and moved partly by political considerations, early in September Göring made a new bid for air superiority by ordering Kesselring to switch his attacks to London. The first attack of the new series, delivered when Park was unavoidably absent from his headquarters, caught the defences at a disadvantage and did heavy damage, but brought Kesselring no decision. Although most of Park's squadrons went into action at one stage or another, the resulting combats did not develop into a major fighter battle with both sides extended to the limit. The air fighting did not go markedly in favour of Kesselring's fighter force, and his bomber losses were substantial.

A second attempt two days later was almost wholly unsuccessful, and again Kesselring suffered fairly heavily. On the other hand, further attacks on September 11 and 14 were ineffectively opposed, and German casualties were deceptively light. But again the results were indecisive.

With his strength substantially reduced by his efforts during the past week, but encouraged by the promise of his last two raids, Kesselring made his final bid on September 15, throwing every available bomber and fighter into two attacks on London in the late morning and early afternoon. Reinforced by his neighbours to left and right, Park committed practically his whole force on each occasion.

During the afternoon raid the long-awaited all-out fighter battle at last took place, about a hundred and eighty of the three hundred fighters put up by Park and his neighbours going into action against roughly the same number of Kesselring's over London and its outskirts while the raid was at its height.

The result was a decision in favour of Park and Dowding and against Kesselring and Göring. Kesselring gained no ascendancy in the fighter battle, and his bomber force was badly mauled. Two days later Hitler, observing that air superiority had not been attained, withheld the preliminary order for invasion and postponed the project 'until further notice'. Next day he ordered that the invasion fleet should be dispersed.

Such, in outline, was the exciting series of events to which the name by which the struggle is known today began to be applied while the fighting was still in progress. During the twenty years that have elapsed a great many accounts of the battle have been written. Few authors have offered a comprehensive explanation of the British victory, and few have tried to assess the military significance of the battle in terms of the principles of strategy and tactics generally held to apply to other battles of like importance.

These omissions are not hard to understand. At first sight the causes of Germany's failure to gain the air superiority needed for invasion seem so various and complex as to defy analysis or even precise statement. Furthermore, in battle not only men's wills but their characters and abilities are matched. Many of the leading actors in the Battle of Britain are still alive; this makes it hard to judge their actions as objectively as if they had fought a century ago. In such crucial decisions as war brings, commanders are often guided as much by instinct as by reason; hence their motives cannot be interpreted except by imputing to them shades of thought and feeling of which they may not be aware, and which they may repudiate. But attempts must be made to overcome these obstacles if the Battle of Britain is not to remain, for the generation that witnessed it, a mere jumble of heroic gestures, utterly unlike any other major battle ever fought, and cut off from the main stream of history.

Among material factors which contributed to Fighter Command's success, by far the most important was a system of early warning and control unparalleled outside Britain. The British had, to say the least, no advantage in numbers, or in the quality of their aircraft, except perhaps as regards the armament of their fighters, which was particularly well suited to its job. The factor which swayed the balance in favour of Dowding's subordinate commanders was the certainty that, except on a few occasions when the system was caught napping, they would be able to position their squadrons in the light of at least a rough-and-ready knowledge of the scale and direction of the enemy's attack. The part played by radar in enabling them to do this has been widely recognised; less attention has been paid to the methods of control, and means of communication, devised in advance of the battle by Dowding and his staff in collaboration with Post Office engineers and others. Combining complexity with simplicity in just the right proportions, these aids to timely interception were not only an outstanding technical feat but also an outstanding example of the kind of preliminary staff work which enables commanders to win battles.

As for moral and personal factors, credit has been rightly given to 'the few'. In the nature of things, not every pilot who flew a Spitfire or a Hurricane was outstanding. To survive the test of combat, a fighter pilot needed something more than the high degree of manual skill which he shared with the driver of a racing car. He needed the physical courage which enables a rugger player to tackle his opponent in the confident expectation that, if anyone gets hurt, it will not be he but the other fellow. He also needed the ability to keep his head in an emergency. Since the last was largely a product of experience, this meant that he needed the luck which alone could bring him safely through his first few combats. Not everyone possessed these gifts in equal measure. The standard of achievement was not uniform throughout the fighter force. Nor was the standard of training, inevitably lowered when dwindling numbers forced the Air Ministry to push newly-fledged pilots into active squadrons as fast as possible. By common consent, the top flight of 'Dowding's chicks', as Winston Churchill called them, were the early birds who were seasoned veterans by the time the fighting reached its climax. Their presence, and their example, made it possible for group and sector commanders to send squadrons into action again and again with complete confidence that they would give a good account of themselves, no matter what the odds.

Even so, no historian, and certainly no one who took an active part in the fighting, would be likely to commit himself to the opinion that pilots and other aircrew on one side or the other were consistently braver and more skilful than their opponents. On the contrary, probably most survivors would agree that, so far as skill and courage in combat were concerned, the two sides were fairly evenly matched—an opinion borne out, to some extent, by the failure of either side to get the upper hand until the Germans were worn down by their attempt to force the pace. What does seem clear is that the side which won was much more intelligently handled by its leaders than the side which lost. Compare Dowding's dogged forethought, his determined husbanding of his resources in defiance of his Government's impulse to disperse them in the vain hope of saving the French Army, with Göring's glib prediction that the air defences of southern England would be eliminated in four days. Compare Park's tactical insight, his providential restraint at times when everything except the instinct of a sound tactician counselled him to risk a gambler's throw, with the facile self-deception which led his opposite number to claim that 'unlimited fighter superiority had been attained' at the very moment when the British were about to fly more fighter sorties between dawn and dusk than they had ever flown before. When these comparisons are made, there cannot be much doubt as to the moral factors which swayed the issue.

Yet Kesselring and Sperrle were not fools or charlatans. They were able men with a wide experience of command and administration in their own service and in the German Army. They began their offensive with so big a preponderance in bombers and fighters that failure must have seemed impossible. Their airmen were brave and skilful, their fighter aircraft of the highest quality, their bombers at least adequate. They had done brilliantly in France and the Low Countries. The task before them when they turned to the attack on England was unfamiliar, but not so unexpected that good information could not be made available about the disposition of the enemy's forces and the location of his most valuable objectives. Why, with all these advantages, did they fail? If one had to answer in a phrase, one could not do it better than by saying that, whereas Dowding and Park proved capable of standing up to men who wanted them to do the wrong things, their German counterparts proved incapable of standing up to Göring.

2

The Stage is Set

ON MONDAY, MAY 20, 1940, Major-General Jodl, Chief of the Operations Staff of the German Supreme Command and Hitler's personal adviser on military questions, noted in his diary that the Führer was 'beside himself with joy'. Ten days from the start of a hazardous offensive against France and the Low Countries, Runstedt's armour had reached the Channel coast, the Franco-British armies were split in two, and Hitler was asking himself what terms he should impose when the French asked for an armistice. Once France had gone the way of Poland, the English could probably be trusted to see reason.

Next day, May 21, Grand-Admiral Raeder, Commander-in-Chief of the German Navy and Head of the Naval War Staff, saw Hitler and raised for the first time at Supreme Headquarters level the question of putting troops ashore on British soil. Raeder did not want a landing in Britain, which all three fighting services had pronounced an almost impossible undertaking unless circumstances were exceptionally favourable. His object was to warn the Führer that the navy would need ample notice if the Supreme Command did decide to land troops instead of trusting to blockade to starve the British out. He learned with relief that 'starvation of the British island empire' by naval and air blockade was still the Führer's policy and that there was no immediate prospect of anything more hazardous.

The stage was set for the Battle of Britain when Hitler departed, in the next few weeks, from the eminently sensible and practical attitude which Raeder found so comforting. The most insistent of the motives which impelled him towards a new standpoint was the earnest wish to be done with the war in the West as soon as possible in order that his long-term aims should not be frustrated by delay. The Moscow Pact, concluded in August, 1939, had made Russia Germany's fellow-conspirator against the peace of Europe. But

Hitler had known for twenty years that it was only at Russia's expense that Germany could find the living-space she claimed, and that Paris was merely the first milestone on the road to the Ukraine. It followed that, sooner or later, he would have to tear up the Moscow Pact and seek in the rich cornlands of Eastern Europe a land fit for the heroes of the Teutonic Master-Race. He now saw that he would have to do it sooner rather than later if he wanted to strike while Russia was still unprepared and the German Army at the peak of its newly-won self-confidence. Yet all his instincts were against a two-front war and he had sworn that he would never fight one. To free his hands for an early attack on Russia he needed a quicker method than blockade of subduing Britain if she obstinately tried to carry on the struggle after France was beaten.

At the end of May and in the first few days of June the bulk of the British Expeditionary Force eluded the Germans at Dunkirk and escaped to England at the cost of leaving most of its heavy equipment on the wrong side of the Channel. Six weeks later Hitler lived up to his reputation for spectacular decisions by ordering the German Army to undertake 'preliminary studies' for an attack on Russia in the autumn—a date soon changed to the spring of 1941. In spite of defiant speeches from his arch-enemy Winston Churchill, he clung meanwhile to the hope that Britain might make peace, but with dwindling conviction in view of reports that Churchill was deter-mined to fight on and would probably carry the country with him.

Towards the end of June Hitler retired to what he was pleased to call his 'battle headquarters' in the Black Forest to draft a final appeal for peace. About the same time Jodl put forward a memo-randum suggesting that the British should be encouraged to take a realistic view of the future by intensified naval and air attacks, to be followed, 'if this were still necessary', by a landing in August or September. Insofar as Hitler was ever influenced by anything but his own hunches—which may, indeed, have been the source of Jodl's inspiration—the arguments in the memorandum were probably decisive. On July 2 the Führer ordered the fighting services to draw up plans for invasion of the United Kingdom. Exactly a fortnight later, after telling the Italian Foreign Minister, Count Ciano, that England would have to be attacked 'with the utmost speed' if the war went on, he announced in a formal directive to the heads of the armed forces that he had 'decided to prepare, and if necessary to carry out', a landing.

No longer beside himself with joy but all too conscious of the gravity of the further decision he might soon have to make, Hitler knew that an invasion bid which fell short of success might end in the worst set-back Germany had experienced since he came to power. Yet so insistent was the need to be done with the West before he turned on Russia that, less than two months after he and Raeder had agreed that blockade was Germany's best weapon, he found himself seriously contemplating the very step which he had then seemed determined to avoid. At the back of his mind, however, was the hope that Britain might yet make peace in time to save him from the awful choice between a two-front war and the perils of an opposed landing in a country which had not been successfully invaded since the combination of a fortunate wind and a well-organised fifth column enabled William of Orange to step triumphantly ashore in Tor Bay in 1688.

Meanwhile the Naval Staff had continued, after Raeder's interview with Hitler on May 21, to study the problem of invasion from the naval point of view. Their studies were intensified in the light of Hitler's order of July 2. The gist of the conclusions which Raeder presented to Hitler on July 11 was that blockade, assisted by air attacks on Liverpool and other centres of distribution, was still the soundest course and that invasion was a desperate remedy which ought to be applied only as a last resort. Once inclined to favour a landing between the Thames and the Tyne if there had to be one anywhere, the Naval Staff now thought that the best hope of getting troops and supplies ashore, without inviting a crushing response from the relatively strong British surface fleet, lay in choosing an area where the voyage would be short and where strong air protection, in addition to defensive minefields on both flanks, could be provided the whole way to the English coast. In effect this meant that, according to the sailors, the crossing would have to be confined to a fairly narrow corridor in or near the Straits of Dover. In any case, said Raeder, he still could not conscientiously advocate invasion unless there were no other way of inducing Britain to sue for peace.

By this time the leaders of the German Army, who had once

5 *Grand-Admiral Raeder, the Naval Commander-in-Chief*

6 *Field-Marshal Kesselring, Commander of Luftflotte 2*

7 *General Halder, Chief of General Staff*

8 *General Stumpff, Commander of Luftflotte 5*

GERMAN COMMANDERS

9 *Field-Marshal Hugo Sperrle, Commander of Luftflotte 3*

10 *Field-Marshal Walter von Brauchitsch, Commander-in-Chief of the German Army*

shared the navy's now-discarded preference for the east coast but had then agreed with the naval planners that in any case a landing was next door to impossible, had not only come round to the view that the south coast was the place but had convinced themselves that invasion was eminently feasible. Only a few days after agreeing once more with Raeder that invasion plans should be put into effect only if all else failed, the Führer was treated to an eager exposition of the army's proposals by Field-Marshal von Brauchitsch, Commander-in-Chief of the German Army. General Halder, the Chief of the General Staff—like Brauchitsch a cautious professional soldier of the old school and a reluctant collaborator with Hitler and his circle—seemed equally sure that the project was at any rate not wildly impractical.

Misinterpreting a statement by the Naval Staff to the effect that the eastern half of the Channel was the best place to cross, the army planners paved the way for further misunderstandings by assuming that troops could be put ashore at points as widely separated as Ramsgate in the east and Lyme Bay in the west. But on one point there was no misunderstanding. Soldiers and sailors agreed that there could be no landing without air superiority over southern England and the English Channel. Hence the crucial question was whether the much-vaunted German Air Force could get the measure of Britain's air defences. Whether the plans of the army and the navy were put into effect would depend on Hitler. Whether they *could* be put into effect would depend on the outcome of a straight fight between Reich Marshal Herman Göring of the Luftwaffe and Air Chief Marshal Sir Hugh Dowding of the Royal Air Force.

Already victorious in Poland, the Luftwaffe had won an immense reputation in recent weeks by its share in the conquest of Denmark, Norway, the Netherlands, Belgium and finally France. The lustre of its triumphs was only fractionally dimmed by the British escape at Dunkirk, because no one could be quite sure—or was ever after-wards to be quite sure—how far the Luftwaffe was to blame.* The self-confident Göring, popularly credited with a big share in the peacetime development of German air power although there is

* 'This is a matter for the Reich Marshal!', Hitler is said to have exclaimed when ways of finishing off the British at Dunkirk were discussed. But most historians blame the German Army for not pressing home its advantage, and the German Army blames Hitler.

some doubt as to the true extent of his contribution, strutted in the limelight of reflected glory.

In the eyes of the elegant Brauchitsch, the conscience-ridden Halder and the painstakingly professional Raeder, Göring was an almost ludicrously repellent figure. His fleshy build, his weakness for gaudy uniforms, his childish vanity and greed made him a laughing-stock to many of his intimates, but not to Hitler, who saw in Göring one of the few men he could trust. Sir Nevile Henderson, the last British Ambassador in Berlin before the war, considered him the least unattractive of the Nazi leaders. In 1917 he had commanded a squadron in the famous Richthofen Geschwader of the original Luftwaffe; some years later he emerged, apparently cured, from a Swedish sanatorium where he was alleged to have been treated for drug-addiction. Self-interest rather than conviction had made him a keen supporter of the Nazi Party, and the Party had brought him wealth and notoriety. As a strategist his chief weakness was the immeasurable self-esteem which prevented him from ack-nowledging that any task could be beyond the capacity of the service he commanded. But this conviction was also a source of strength. With all his faults, Göring was not a man who would readily admit defeat.

Except that the last could be said also of his opponent, the two men could hardly have been more dissimilar. A Wykehamist and the son of a Wykehamist, Sir Hugh Dowding was a thoughtful man with a highly individual cast of mind. A varied experience of service life, which included a long spell as a subaltern in India, had armoured him against the nagging doubts which often inhibit action in men brought up to think. He knew the value of decision. A deeply but unconventionally religious man, he inherited from both sides of his family a keen sense of responsibility towards his fellow-creatures. Aware that his principles were sound, he was seldom in much doubt as to what was right for them and him. Before taking control of the air defences in 1936 he had, for six crucial years, been responsible for framing the policy of the Royal Air Force in matters of research and technical development: under his guidance the service had begun the shift from the slow wooden biplane to the fast all-metal monoplane, from old-fashioned sound locators and other primitive devices to methods of long-range detection which were still a closely-guarded secret. Now, in 1940, he felt as if he had been preparing all his life for the battle which he knew was coming. In May, before it began, he laid the foundations of victory by arguing the Prime Minister, Winston Churchill, out of his generous inclination to sacrifice the fighter force in a vain attempt to save France from defeat. With his unrivalled experience, his technical background, his tenacity in debate and his burning faith, he was probably the only man in England who could have done it.

Across the Channel, Hitler's directive of July 16 brought an energetic response from the German Army. On the 17th Brauchitsch ordered thirteen picked divisions to the Channel coast. By early August all were in position and were training systematically for the invasion project, henceforth known as Operation Sealion.

Meanwhile a reign of terror was being prepared for conquered Britain. A certain S.S. Colonel Professor Dr. Six, afterwards a member of the organisation responsible for large-scale massacres in Russia, was designated Representative of the Chief of the Security Police and Security Services in Great Britain; lists were drawn up of Members of Parliament, artists, writers and other public figures who were to be imprisoned or detained; notices were printed in English and German, forbidding unauthorised entry to requisitioned buildings. Later, orders were drafted for the deportation to the Continent of all able-bodied male civilians between the ages of seventeen and forty-five whom the authorities succeeded in arresting.

In the nature of things, naval preparations went more slowly. In the light of the army's estimate of the troops needed for invasion, the Naval Staff calculated that more than a hundred and fifty large transports, about seventeen hundred barges and nearly as many tugs, motor-boats and trawlers would be needed to carry even the so-called first wave across the Channel within ten days of the start. To assemble such a fleet was a gigantic undertaking which Raeder undertook reluctantly and with dire prophecies of the effect on Germany's economy.

To make the picture even gloomier, a fundamental misunderstanding between the army and the navy came to light at the end of July. When Halder found that the Naval Staff had never contemplated landings on a broad front in the eastern half of the Channel, but merely that troops should land on a narrow one somewhere within that area, he spoke disgustedly of 'throwing away the whole plan of an invasion'. Ultimately, however, he and Brauchitsch accepted a compromise dictated by the realities of the naval situation. If the ships were ready in time, if the Luftwaffe gained air superiority, and if Hitler decided to take the plunge, then troops of the Sixteenth and Ninth Armies under Generals Busch and Strauss, supplemented by paratroops dropped near Folkestone, would do their best to get ashore on a series of narrow fronts on either side of Beachy Head from Hythe to Rottingdean. If they succeeded, they would push forward to hold a bridgehead from Brighton through Uckfield, Tenterden and Ashford to the coast of Thanet. Once firmly established, the two armies would extend the bridgehead to cover practically the whole of Kent and Sussex and parts of the adjacent counties. Only if all went well, and perhaps not even then, would two divisions of the Sixth Army under Field-Marshal von Reichenau land later in Lyme Bay and join in a concerted advance to a line across the breadth of England from the Blackwater to the Severn.

Although one effect of these changes was to reduce the number of barges needed for the landing, the navy's task remained so formidable that invasion still seemed to Raeder a desperate venture. At the same time the confidence of the army's leaders was shaken by the restriction of their front, so that they, too, came to regard the project as hardly feasible unless the stuffing could be knocked out of the enemy by the time the troops were asked to administer the *coup de grâce*. Hence the role of the Luftwaffe became more than ever vital. Even if Göring's airmen defeated the Royal Air Force and stopped the Royal Navy from sinking the invasion fleet, the landing might still fail unless they could also crush resistance by preventing the British from moving reserves towards the lodgment area.

It was characteristic of Göring that he did not shrink from this monstrously tall order. It was also characteristic that the basis of his confidence was not that he really thought that he could eliminate even a poorly-equipped British Army after knocking out the Royal Air Force and checkmating the Royal Navy, but that he did not expect to have to do it. Sharing with many airmen in all countries wildly exaggerated notions of the effectiveness of air attack, he believed that a display of ruthless might would be so decisive that German troops would be able to land with practically no opposition. Since this was exactly what Brauchitsch and Halder hoped might happen, they saw little reason to challenge Göring's views as long as it was possible to believe that he might not be mistaken.

Whether he could drive the Royal Air Force from the skies—in which case the rest would follow—was thus for Göring not merely the crucial question but almost the only question worth considering. Nor had he much doubt about the answer. In effect his object would be attained if the air defences were knocked out, since the aerodromes and factories on which the rest of the Royal Air Force depended could then be destroyed at leisure. Four days, thought Göring, should be enough to smash the air defences of southern England, four weeks to complete the job.

In the light of the factors known to Göring, this opinion was not quite as fatuous as it seems in retrospect. Except at Dunkirk, the Luftwaffe had carried all before it in recent weeks. A staggering array of military aerodromes, all with fairly good communications and many conveniently close to England, had fallen into German hands. Thanks to a mobility unknown in other air forces, the Luftwaffe was able to fly from them almost as soon as they were captured. Bombs and fuel were plentiful. Less than a month after the fall of France, the German Air Force was on the starting line for its next dash to victory. All Göring needed before he could fire the gun was a little time to draw up plans, allot targets and brief crews.

Numerically, too, the Luftwaffe was very strong. A month after the French surrender, Göring had fifteen hundred bombers and more than a thousand fighters in France and the Low Countries, besides much smaller numbers in Scandinavia. His intelligence officers assessed Air Chief Marshal Dowding's resources, fairly accurately, at fifty squadrons of Hurricanes and Spitfires with a first-line strength of roughly nine hundred aircraft and a tactical strength of six hundred. Since Dowding had the whole of the United Kingdom to defend, while the Luftwaffe could attack at points of its own choosing, Göring had some warrant for the hope that he could overwhelm his enemy by sheer weight of numbers.

But these figures did not tell the whole story. About a fifth of Göring's striking force consisted of dive-bombers, useful for attacking weakly-defended targets or terrorising inadequately-trained troops, but slow, vulnerable and with a painfully small radius of action. A good many of the fighters were long-range machines which could never be a match for Hurricanes and Spitfires.

Except where unescorted or weakly escorted bombers could be risked, the extent of the Luftwaffe's operations over Britain would be governed by the size and scope of its short-range fighter force. The number of short-range fighters available on a given day was not likely to be more than seven hundred, and their radius of action was about a hundred miles. On the assumption that at least two fighters were needed to protect one bomber, this meant that, as long as the British fighter force was undefeated, full-scale operations in daylight would be limited to attacks by not more than three or four hundred bombers at a time on objectives south and east of a line from Weymouth to Ipswich. The question Göring ought to have asked himself was not whether Dowding, with fifty day-fighter squadrons and seventeen hundred anti-aircraft guns at his disposal, could take on two thousand five hundred German bombers and fighters, but whether he could take on the thousand or so which were all the Luftwaffe could expect to put against him at one time.

It is improbable that Göring did ask himself that question. Like many a commander before his time, he tended not only to under-estimate his enemy but to overlook facts which were not thrust before his eyes. He ignored or undervalued the cardinal features of Dowding's strength, not because no information about them was available, but because they were not obvious, and what was not obvious did not interest him. The strength of Britain's air defences did not lie only in such things as the skill of pilots and gunners and the performance of guns and aircraft. British fighter pilots were superlatively well trained; but so were their opponents. The British monoplane fighter, as exemplified by the Hurricane and Spitfire, was a magnificent gun-platform; but German designers and technicians, profiting, as in 1914, from experience gained in international motor-car racing, had produced in the Messerschmitt 109 a short-range fighter superior in all-round performance to the Hurricane and in some ways superior to the Spitfire. British anti-aircraft gunners were keen, and so was their Commander-in-Chief, Lieutenant-General Sir Frederick Pile; but Pile had fewer than half the guns to which he was entitled, and much of his ancillary equipment was hopelessly old-fashioned. The factor which enormously increased the value of every one of Dowding's squadrons, and which Göring failed to take into account, was that a system of early warning and control, unequalled outside Britain, enabled him and his subordinate commanders to keep track of approaching aircraft and put fighters in the right position to intercept them. This was the hidden weapon—a weapon hidden only in the sense that Göring hardly troubled to consider it, although his subordinates knew of its existence—which might well turn the scale in Dowding's favour even if he were heavily outnumbered. And it was this little-noticed asset which justified the Chiefs of Staff in telling the Prime Minister, when things looked blackest, that the country had a good chance of survival.

3

The Hidden Weapon

THE ORIGIN OF the Fighter Command system of early warning and control goes back to the closing months of the First World War, when air defence was the business of the army and the London Air Defence Area was commanded by Major-General E. B. Ashmore, a gunner who understood the ways of airmen and was well served by his handful of fighter squadrons.

General Ashmore was an able and popular officer with a wide experience as gunner and air defence commander. By the time he left the service his knowledge of anti-aircraft gunnery was unsurpassed. After his retirement he published a book on air defence which must have been among the first written on the subject in any language.

In the summer of 1918 Ashmore and his staff developed a method of displaying information about the movements of hostile aircraft by means of coloured counters on a huge map in a central operations room at the Horse Guards in Whitehall. The information was fed by landline through more or less devious channels from distant listening-posts. Other landlines connected the operations room with the various components of air defence. The essence of the system was that it enabled an officer sitting in an armchair in London to deal with an enemy he never saw by sending up fighters from an aerodrome many miles away, and even to give orders to pilots in the air by means of a rudimentary form of radio-telephony.

By the time the system was perfected, Ashmore and his team had gained such an ascendancy that no German aircraft ventured near enough for them to try it, in its final form, against a real enemy. Nevertheless its performance in exercises convinced them that it would at least double the effectiveness of the defences. This was saying a good deal since, even without the perfected system, Ashmore's command had achieved a rate of destruction which few air forces could stand indefinitely.

The London Air Defence Area was abolished soon after the

Armistice; but the system was not forgotten, and Ashmore was called in when the air defences were revived in the 1920s. His experience underlined the importance of first-class communications and centralised control. It was obvious that, in a future war, the air defences could not afford to rely, as they had done in the past, on messages laboriously passed from listening-post to local police-station, from local police-station to district police-headquarters, from district police-headquarters to the metropolitan police in London, and thence at last to the commander whose swift response meant the difference between success and failure. As the new scheme took shape, and especially after its recasting in the 1930s to meet the threat from Germany, provision of a landline network to meet the ever-more-exacting demands of airmen became a major job for Post Office engineers and planners.

But even the time saved by reducing lags in transmission would not make the system effective unless the information itself was timely. Unfortunately, as the speed of aircraft increased, it soon ceased to be so. By the early 1930s the warning given by listening-posts on the coast had become too short for fighters to be put up with any chance of intercepting an enemy before he reached an objective as near as London. Various alternatives to sound-location—for example, detection of the heat emitted by an internal combustion engine rather than of the noise it made—were considered but dismissed as unpromising. Almost in desperation, the Air Ministry collaborated with the War Office in building huge curved mirrors—one of them, at Hythe in Kent, was two hundred feet long—to reflect the sound to the usual amplifiers. These outsize sound-detectors, or 'acoustic mirrors', proved unsatisfactory, largely because the amplifiers had to be turned inland to face them, and thus tended to pick up the roar of nearby traffic more readily than the faint, reflected hum of the distant target aircraft. For years the problem seemed insoluble—so insoluble that Stanley Baldwin predicted with devastating candour in 1932 that 'the bomber would always get through'.

This verdict chimed well with the opinion of many airmen that the bomber was the invincible weapon of the future and perhaps even of the present. Nevertheless there were men both inside and outside the Royal Air Force and the Air Ministry who refused to believe that the bomber would always get through and that there was no prospect of intercepting hostile aircraft at least often enough to make bombing hazardous. Air Chief Marshal Sir Robert Brooke-Popham, commanding the moribund air defences and chairman of a committee which was studying their reorganisation to meet the changed conditions of the Hitler era, did not despair of progress if some better means of early warning could be found than sound-locators which smacked of an age of wooden biplanes. H. T. Tizard, Chairman of the Aeronautical Research Committee, and H. E. Wimperis, Director of Scientific Research at the Air Ministry, were all too keenly aware of the need to replace acoustic methods by new devices. From the more detached standpoint of Oxford, F. A. Lindemann, an old friend of Tizard's but the confidant of the Air Ministry's severest critic, Winston Churchill, shared the view that a new solution must be found. The question was whether Tizard and Wimperis were capable of finding it.

In the end they did, though not without going outside the Air Ministry for the answer. The initiative came from Wimperis. Towards the end of 1934 he suggested that a committee under Tizard should be set up to review all possible solutions, among them some hitherto rejected as too far-fetched for serious consideration. The new committee, called the Committee for the Scientific Survey of Air Defence, held its first meeting on January 28, 1935. Almost, but not quite, simultaneously, pressure from outside the Air Ministry led to the setting up of an Air Defence Research Sub-Committee of the Committee of Imperial Defence for the purpose of surveying much the same field at the inter-service level.

Before the first meeting of the Committee for the Scientific Survey of Air Defence, and in preparation for it, Wimperis asked R. A. (afterwards Sir Robert) Watson-Watt of the National Physical Laboratory at Teddington whether there was any chance of using something akin to the 'death-ray' of science fiction to destroy hostile aircraft or harm their occupants. In theory, such an application of electro-magnetic radiations was not utterly beyond the realm of the possible; but Watson-Watt reported that it would not work in practice. In any case, said Watson-Watt, the first step was to detect and locate the quarry; if the Air Ministry were interested in doing that, he might be able to suggest something that would help. After spending years detecting and locating thunderstorms for the benefit of the Meteorological Office, largely with equipment of his own devising, he was now using similar equipment to determine the distance from the earth of the phenomenon known as the Heaviside layer or ionosphere. He suspected that radio waves, which bounced back from thunderstorms and the ionosphere, would also bounce back from an aircraft. If they did, a minimum of two combined transmitting and receiving stations, suitably placed and using his method of noting the time taken by a radio pulse to travel to the objective and back, would suffice to establish the aircraft's plan position. If a means could then be found of determining the aircraft's height as well, the problem of detection and location would be solved.

The Committee for the Scientific Survey of Air Defence duly held their first meeting, invited Watson-Watt to follow up his suggestion, and arranged that the Air Member for Research and Development should be asked to find funds for the project. Dowding, interested but sceptical, called first for evidence that Watson-Watt's idea would work. On February 26 Watson-Watt gave a demonstration with the aid of a Heyford aircraft and the B.B.C.'s transmitter at Daventry, and Dowding was convinced. A substantially larger sum than Tizard had asked for was provided, and an experimental station was set up on the Suffolk coast at Orfordness. Within a few months aircraft were being detected up to forty miles away, and acoustic mirrors were as dead as mutton.

By the summer of 1936, when Dowding left the Air Ministry to take up his new job at the head of the new air defence organisation, the first of a series of soaring metal towers, as tall as cathedral spires, which sprang up round the coast in the last few years of peace, had taken its place as a familiar feature of the local landscape after giving its constructors many anxious moments. The Air Ministry did something to satisfy curiosity without giving too much away by calling the new installations Radio Direction-Finding stations, and by telling enquirers, with literal accuracy, that they were connected with Watson-Watt's ionosphere experiments. The Germans fathomed the purpose of the stations, and sent the airship *Graf Zeppelin* to take a look at them, but underrated their performance, believing that users would be unable to distinguish between large raids and small and could easily be kept guessing by diversionary attacks.

As headquarters of the new defensive system the Air Ministry chose an almost derelict mansion at Stanmore, in the north-western suburbs about twelve miles from Charing Cross. Until the eve of the transformation which swept away the old Air Defence of Great Britain command and its ancillary formations, the place had been in use as headquarters of the command called Inland Area. Formerly it had been a girls' school and, before that, a hotel. In the days of its glory a noted host, the Marquess of Abercorn, had made it, according to Lady Blessington, 'the most singular place on earth, where everyone is invited the moment they become celebrated'. Later a less expansive figure, the Dowager Queen Adelaide, leased the house and grounds and lived there from 1846 until her death. The property owed its name, Bentley Priory, to an ancient religious foundation whose crumbling ruins continued to occupy the site until the second half of the eighteenth century. After many ups and downs the new house, now growing old, was about to qualify once more for Lady Bessington's tribute, though not quite for the old reason. Before long there would again be no place on earth with a better claim to be called unique than Bentley Priory.

At nine o'clock in the morning on July 14, 1936, Dowding presented himself at Bentley Priory to take up his new job. It was characteristic of the man that he arrived unaccompanied and without fuss. At the same time it was symptomatic of his future relations with the Air Council, of which he had just ceased to be a distinguished member, that the Air Ministry had not sent anyone to welcome him. Nor, apparently, had they warned anyone that he was coming. Dowding's staff had not arrived. The Camp Commandant was away. The Air Officer Commanding-in-Chief, after satisfying the guard of his identity, was shown round his headquarters by the N.C.O. in charge of the Orderly Room.

Except that the gardens were well kept, the place had obviously gone down hill since the days when Pitt and Wellington and Nelson, and Sydney Smith and Theodore Hook and Sheridan, showed their paces in the big-windowed drawing-room overlooking Harrow Weald. Designed, and afterwards remodelled, by Sir John Soane in a heavily frolicsome style which mingled vaguely classical proportions with a touch of Gothic gloom and a dash of oriental fantasy, the building cried out for overtones of bustle and movement to redeem its sombreness. Too long unoccupied before Inland Area took it over, too long abandoned to makeshift uses, it bore the

11 *The 300-foot mast of a Radar Station*

12 *In the operations room of a Sector Station*

THE HIDDEN WEAPON

13   Mr. H. T. (*later Sir Henry*) *Tizard, Chairman of the Aeronautical Research Committee, 1933–43*

14   Mr. R. A. (*later Sir Robert*) *Watson Watt, British pioneer of Radar*

15   *Lord Beaverbrook, Minister of Aircraft Production, 1940–41*

16   *Sir Kingsley Wood, Secretary of State for Air, 1938–40*

BRITISH SCIENTISTS AND STATESMEN

marks of a habitation which has ceased to be a home and become an institution. The basement, as Dowding remarked, smelled damp.

But the situation was superb. To the south the landscape fell away in a succession of wooded slopes which hid the western suburbs. On clear days the Surrey Hills, nearly thirty miles away beyond the Thames, were just visible, their faint blue outline almost masked by the nearer heights of Harrow. To the south-east, obscured by a haze which no one had yet learnt to call smog, lay the crowded mass of inner London, a clutter of tempting targets for enterprising bomber crews.

From this point of vantage Dowding surveyed the immense task of remodelling the air defences of Great Britain to meet a threat unforeseen when the foundations of the system were laid in the 1920s. Until recently the shaping of the defences had been governed by the assumption that France was the potential enemy, not because anyone expected France to attack Britain, but because she was the strongest Continental power, and for long the only one whose bombers could reach London. A start had been made with a new layout designed to meet the threat from Germany, but no more than a start. Then, too, the weapons which the new system must exploit were not only still untried, but were utterly unlike any which could have been conceived a few years earlier. The aircraft which Dowd--ing's squadrons would have by the time they were fit for war were not yet in squadron service, and were so different from existing types in feel and performance that hitherto only a handful of picked pilots had been reckoned capable of flying them. The new early-warning devices were revolutionary to a degree which put them almost past belief. Even the guns which the hard-used anti-aircraft gunners hoped to get by the time war broke out were largely of new design. Almost the only thing that was not new was the principle of centralised control bequeathed by Ashmore.

In this situation Dowding's technical bent, and the familiarity with recent developments which his long spell at the Air Ministry had given him, were of immense value. To apply Ashmore's principle to conditions which Ashmore could never have imagined was a job that suited Dowding. He tackled it with quiet relish. He found in Air Vice-Marshal Keith Park, the lean, athletic New Zealander who soon became his Senior Air Staff Officer, a right-hand man with a mind attuned to his, although the two men were not alike in temperament.

Gradually the new organisation took shape as ideas were tried out and discarded or adopted. The essence of the system was the centralisation of the early-warning complex at Bentley Priory and the devolution of tactical control to subordinate formations. From a score and more of R.D.F. stations round the coast—they were not called radar stations until the middle of the war—messages reached Bentley Priory through telephones constantly manned from the moment when war seemed imminent. As fast as it could be spoken, the news that hostile or unidentified aircraft were approaching, with such details of height and numbers as the equipment could provide, came in from tiny hutted camps on windswept moors, from the grounds of a Victorian mansion in Suffolk, from Stenigot and High Street and a dozen other sites whose names might have been chosen expressly to baffle the enemy, but were in fact simply those of the nearest village or convenient landmark. At Dowding's headquarters the information was sifted, or 'filtered', emerging as a map reference to which was added a number by which the corresponding aircraft or formation of aircraft continued to be designated as long as it remained within the ken of the defences. From the filter room, at first in the house but later underground, the filtered information, or 'plot', was 'told' simultaneously to the command operations room a few yards away and to the operations rooms of appropriate subordinate formations throughout the country. In each operations room a number of plotters, wearing headphones and armed with magnetic wands resembling fishing-rods, traced the course of the aircraft or formation on the operations table with coloured counters, switching from one colour to another at fixed intervals so that 'stale' plots could be distinguished from fresh ones.

In a sense the early-warning system was thus both centralised and decentralised. It was centralised inasmuch as the crude information from R.D.F. stations came only to Command Headquarters—an arrangement abandoned later, when the number of R.D.F. stations became too great for one filter room to deal with all of them. It was decentralised inasmuch as the useful, filtered information reached lower formations just as soon as it reached the command operations room.

As soon as an approaching aircraft crossed the coast, responsibility for keeping track of it passed from the R.D.F. stations to observer posts. These were too numerous to report straight to Command Headquarters. They passed their information to observer centres, which passed it on to operations rooms.

So much for the tracking of hostile or unidentified aircraft approaching the country or flying over it. When it came to engaging them with fighters or anti-aircraft guns, centralised control from Command Headquarters was out of the question. Even in the comparatively leisurely atmosphere of 1918, General Ashmore had not been expected to control a nation-wide system from Whitehall. Had German aircraft attacked the north of England, a separate Northern Air Defence Area would have gone into action.

At first Dowding's command was sub-divided into two groups covering the north and south of England. By the summer of 1940 there were four groups, each in turn sub-divided into a number of sectors. No. 11 Group, with headquarters at Uxbridge, covered London and south-east England. No. 12 Group, with headquarters at Watnall, near Nottingham, looked after the Eastern Counties and the Midlands. Nominally No. 13 Group's province extended over the north of England, the whole of Scotland, and as far west as Northern Ireland, but cover was incomplete in many parts of this vast area. Group Headquarters were at Newcastle. No. 10 Group, an addition tentatively planned before the war, begun in February, 1940, and brought hurriedly into action when France fell, covered the West Country, had its headquarters at Rudloe, near Bath, and enjoyed the privilege, then unique, of doing its own filtering. Until the end of the first week in August No. 10 Group commanded only three sectors with headquarters at Pembrey in South Wales, St. Eval in Cornwall, and Filton near Exeter; but it then took over from No. 11 Group the Middle Wallop sector, whose boundaries corresponded roughly with those of Wiltshire and Dorset. Thereafter No. 11 Group, with sector stations at Tangmere, Kenley, Biggin Hill, Hornchurch, Northolt, North Weald and Debden, was responsible for the defence of London and the south-eastern counties from Hampshire to Suffolk; No. 12 Group, with sector stations at Duxford, Coltishall, Wittering, Digby, Kirton-in-Lindsey and Church Fenton, for the rest of England as far north as Whitby. No. 13 Group covered as much of its enormous territory as it could

Group Boundaries
- - - Sector Boundaries
⊙ Sector Stations
⟨IAZ⟩ London Inner Artillery Zone

Wick ⊙

Turnhouse ⊙

No.13 GROUP
(SAUL)

Acklington ⊙

Usworth ⊙

Aldergrove ⊙

Catterick ⊙

No.12 GROUP
(LEIGH-MALLORY)

Church Fenton ⊙

Kirton-in-Lindsey ⊙

Digby ⊙

Wittering ⊙

Coltishall ⊙

Duxford ⊙

Debden ⊙

N. Weald ⊙

Pembrey ⊙

Northolt ⊙ ⟨IAZ⟩ Hornchurch ⊙

Filton ⊙

Biggin Hill ⊙

Kenley ⊙

M. Wallop ⊙

Tangmere ⊙

No. 10 GROUP
(BRAND)

No. 11 GROUP
(PARK)

St. Eval ⊙

0   50   100

Miles

—ARTHUR BANKS—

17 *Organisation of Fighter Command, August, 1940*

from sector stations at Catterick, Usworth and Acklington in the north of England, Turnhouse, Dyce and Wick in Scotland, and Aldergrove in Northern Ireland.

Broadly, the system of interception as it existed throughout the battle was that Command Headquarters, once it had done its filtering and ordered the sounding of public air-raid warnings, made no further contribution to the tactical situation. Executive orders were given by groups and sectors. Groups decided which of their sectors should deal with a given raid approaching their area of responsibility or flying over it, and told sectors what forces to put into the air or bring to readiness. Once fighters were airborne, sectors were responsible for giving orders which would put them in the right position to engage the enemy. Anti-aircraft guns were tied into the system by direct landlines connecting Group Head-quarters with gun operations rooms, which in turn were linked with gun sites; searchlights were linked through troop and battery headquarters with sector stations.

As it was manifestly impossible for the same people to be on duty all the time, operations rooms were continuously manned on a watchkeeping basis, and group and sector commanders were represented by duty controllers who dealt with situations as they arose. Thus it was normally from the duty group controller that orders to put up aircraft reached a sector operations room, and from the sector controller that the leader of a squadron, flight or section learned what was expected of him and where the enemy was thought to be. At the same time, group and sector commanders usually took care to be present when an important action was in progress, and often gave decisions on the spot.*

Complex in structure, the system worked with admirable simplicity. Practical difficulties in interception arose chiefly from lags in transmission and inaccurate estimates of height. Even at best an

* In accordance with the well-established principle that commanding officers are responsible for the authorised acts of their staffs and deputies, and for the sake of simplicity and clarity, the convention has been adopted in the account that follows of attributing important tactical decisions to the responsible commanders, even though it is obvious that, on many occasions, the relevant order must have been given by subordinates. An exception has been made in dealing with the events of September 7, where some historical interest attaches to the known fact that Air Vice-Marshal Park was unavoidably absent from his headquarters when the first daylight raid was made on London.

enemy formation was likely to be from twelve to twenty miles ahead of the position shown on operations tables, for it took about four minutes for information from R.D.F. stations to be digested at the source, passed on, filtered, told to operations rooms and plotted, and roughly the same time for reports from observer posts to go through the corresponding process. This discrepancy could be allowed for, and was not a very big handicap as long as controllers acted promptly.

The problem of height was not so easily overcome. Estimation of height was not one of R.D.F.'s strongest points, and even experienced members of the Observer Corps sometimes made mistakes or were baffled by the weather. The consequence was that controllers tended to rely as much on experience of the enemy's habits as on the figures displayed in operations rooms, and that formation leaders sometimes went one better by disbelieving what controllers told them. On the whole intelligent anticipation gave good results, but occasionally, in cloudy weather, enemy formations were missed when they might conceivably have been intercepted had the original estimates been taken at their face value. A point not always grasped by critics of the system was that controllers had to allow a quarter of an hour or more for squadrons to reach the height at which the enemy was likely to be found, and were naturally reluctant to risk sending them in so low that they might be jumped upon.

In the thick of the battle fighter pilots tended, in the nature of things, to be more conscious of the shortcomings of the system than of its merits. A few, though seldom the best or the most experienced, were inclined to ridicule the whole business, regarding controllers as armchair tacticians hopelessly out of touch with reality, and attributing all successful interceptions solely to their own skill and that of their formation leaders. The point they overlooked was that, without the system, there would have been no interceptions at all except on prohibitive terms, so that all their skill and courage would have gone for nothing. Had lack of an early-warning and control system forced Dowding to rely on standing patrols, most of his squadrons would have been worn to a standstill long before Göring launched his main assault. Whether, in that case, overwhelming air superiority would have enabled the Germans to land without naval superiority is an open question. One thing certain is that, had they succeeded in establishing and consolidating a bridgehead, the

British Army, inexperienced in mobile warfare and with hardly any armour or anti-tank guns, could not have stopped their further advance. Unless thrown back into the sea in the first few days, General Strauss's troops could have been in London in six weeks.

4

Undreamt-of Might

'I have done my best to make the German Air Force ready to carry out every command of the Führer with lightning speed and undreamt-of might.'   *Herman Göring*

THE GERMAN ORGANISATION for the air attack on Britain changed little, except in minor respects, throughout the battle. As its shortcomings were partly responsible for the German defeat, it deserves a little study.

The highest Luftwaffe formation outside the Air Ministry was the Luftflotte, or air fleet, a command of varying size and importance whose subordinate formations sometimes comprised a number of air corps or air divisions, and sometimes only one. The air corps and air divisions in turn were of no fixed size, their establishment depending on the Air Ministry's assessment of their needs. A characteristic feature of the Luftwaffe, and one of the secrets of its exceptional mobility, was that tremendous pains were taken to relieve flying units of much of the donkey-work of administration and supply. Besides the air corps or air divisions, which looked after operations, each Luftflotte comprised a number of district commands concerned solely with supply and maintenance, and working through subordinate formations which covered every operational aerodrome in German hands. While the system was working well and while supplies were plentiful, a flying unit arriving on a strange aerodrome could thus be sure that it would find everything it needed, or could get it quickly.

The chief tactical formations in the Luftwaffe were the Staffel, or squadron, of nine aircraft, and the Gruppe, or wing, of three squadrons. In general, three operational Gruppen, with the addition of a headquarters flight and a reserve or training Gruppe, made up a Geschwader—a formation with no exact equivalent in any other service, but intended to stand in roughly the same relation to its component units as a cavalry regiment does to troops and squadrons.

The designation of every bomber and fighter wing and squadron in the Luftwaffe, except a few independent Gruppen and some specialist units, by the number of its parent Geschwader and an identifying prefix, suggests that the framers of the system meant the Geschwader to be the focus of tradition. But detachment of a Gruppe from its Geschwader was so common that the ability of Gruppen to work independently was vital. The German squadron, on the other hand, was a good deal less self-contained than its British counterpart.

One of the most curious features of the system, and a potent source of weakness, was the extreme sketchiness of the intelligence organisation in the field. This was not due to the shortcomings of the German secret service, which were more apparent on the political than on the military side. Notwithstanding a tendency to misspell English names and impute sinister functions to such blameless institutions as the Church of England and the Boy Scout Movement, German intelligence officers at the higher levels were not unskilful and were usually fairly well informed about matters of operational significance. Where the system broke down so far as the Luftwaffe was concerned was in the poverty of the arrangements for disseminating information to lower formations and making sure that it was understood and used. The Luftwaffe made no provision for full-time intelligence officers below Geschwader level. Aircrews thus depended for their knowledge of the enemy on their own observations in the heat of battle, supplemented by such garbled intelligence as reached them from superior formations through the medium of an adjutant or operations officer without special training and preoccupied with more immediate concerns. Not surprisingly, prisoners of war were sometimes so ignorant of conditions outside German-occupied territory, and so bemused by propaganda emanating from Hitler and his circle, that they were utterly bowled over by their first contact with English life. This limitation is particularly worth noting in view of a tendency to credit surviving German commanders of relatively junior rank with an all-round knowledge of events, and an insight into the minds of their superiors, which no one would think of ascribing to their counterparts on this side of the Channel.

At the end of the campaign in France and the Low Countries the two air fleets which had done so well in recent weeks were deployed

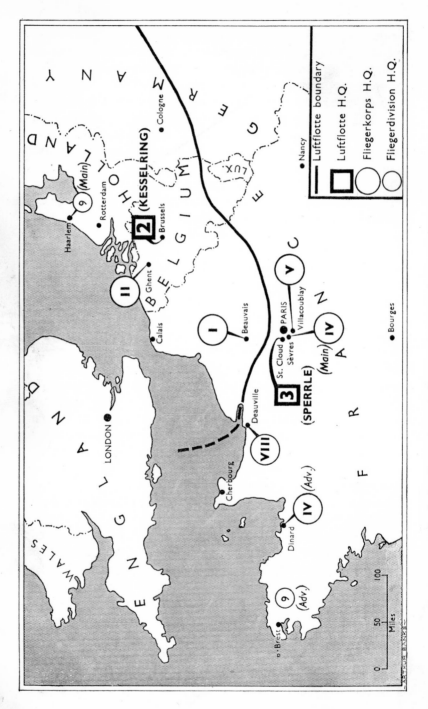

18 Luftwaffe organization in France and the Low Countries. S...

from the Netherlands to Brest on a front of about five hundred miles. Luftflotte 2, with headquarters in Brussels, commanded two air corps and an independent air division with their respective headquarters at Beauvais, Ghent and Haarlem. The Luftflotte commander, Field-Marshal Kesselring, was a fifty-four-year-old former artillery officer who had served on the General Staff in the First World War and had made his name as an administrator. In the summer of 1940 he had behind him not only the experience of the battle just concluded, but also that of the campaign in Poland, in which he had played a leading part.

Field-Marshal Sperrle, commanding Luftflotte 3 on Kesselring's left flank, was a few months older, had switched from the infantry to the flying service in his early thirties, and had commanded the German air contingent in the Spanish Civil War. Both he and Kesselring had been on the staff of the German Ministry of Defence in the days just after the First World War when the revived Luftwaffe was only an aspiration in the minds of a few ambitious men who chafed at Germany's defeat. His headquarters were at Saint-Cloud, on the western outskirts of Paris. Within a few minutes' drive, at Villacoublay and Sèvres respectively, were the headquarters of one of his three air corps and the rear headquarters of another whose advanced headquarters were at Dinard. The remaining corps was based on Deauville.

For the purpose of the battle the boundary between the two Luftflotten, which followed the course of the Seine from Paris to Le Havre, was extended across the Channel to Selsey Bill, whence it ran just west of Oxford and Birmingham and just east of Manchester to the Pennine watershed on the borders of Lancashire and Yorkshire. Other preparations for the attack on Britain included the setting up in each Luftflotte of a makeshift organisation for the co-ordination of attacks on shipping, and the grouping of fighter units in special sub-commands to simplify co-operation with striking forces. These sub-commands came into their own when the Luftwaffe was forced on to the defensive and could not do without a system of ground-control which emulated, but never equalled, the British system.

Between them Kesselring and Sperrle disposed of the entire operational strength of twelve complete and three incomplete long-range bomber Geschwader, besides four independent Gruppen, the whole with a first-line strength of nearly thirteen hundred aircraft. Just under a third of the bombers were Junkers 88s, the fastest and best German bombers yet introduced to service but still unpopular with aircrew because they were reputed difficult to handle; the rest were more or less obsolescent Heinkel 111s and Dornier 17s. In addition the two Luftflotten had about three hundred dive-bombers, slow and vulnerable Junkers 87s. About eight hundred Messerschmitt 109s, comprising eight entire Geschwader and elements from two more, made up the combined short-range fighter force; fewer than three hundred unsatisfactory Messerschmitt 110s its long-range counterpart. Reconnaissance aircraft, minelaying seaplanes and a few night-fighters brought the overall strength of Kesselring's and Sperrle's commands to a figure not far short of three thousand aircraft—nearly half as much again as the entire first-line strength of the Royal Air Force at the beginning of the war. On the other hand the number of *serviceable* aircraft in the two Luftflotten never exceeded about two-thirds of that figure, even with the inclusion of types not used in the battle or soon withdrawn because they could not stand the pace.

General Stumpff, commanding Luftflotte 5 in Denmark and Norway, was far less generously equipped. He had had his hour of glory in the spring, when his single air corps played a vital part in the Scandinavian campaign, but had since been shorn of more than half his strength. His striking force on the eve of the battle consisted of fewer than a hundred and fifty long-range bombers belonging to two incomplete Geschwader afterwards transferred to Kesselring. These were adequate for the carefully-rehearsed attacks on shipping off the coasts of Scotland and England as far south as the Humber which were Stumpff's contribution to the blockade, but were bound to suffer heavily in attacks on inland targets unless well escorted. Towards the two or three hundred high-performance long-range fighters needed to escort them, Stumpff had thirty-seven Messerschmitt 110s. This deficiency, made only slightly less painful by the knowledge that even ten times as many Messerschmitt 110s would not have solved his problem, he owed to the muddled belief of his superiors that he could, at one and the same time, draw off some of Dowding's fire for the benefit of his neighbours to the south and carve a way for his own striking force.

Apart from the faulty disposition which sprang from this misapprehension, the Germans were handicapped by failure to under-stand the nature and extent of the task ahead of them. Reluctance to face facts was not the prerogative of any one service or any one country, but it ran right through the Luftwaffe, and was particularly glaring at the higher levels. In France and the Low Countries the Germans had astonished their enemies by the excellence of the machinery they had devised for the rapid summoning of air support to troops. This was precisely the task for which the leaders of the Luftwaffe, discarding the doctrine of the strategic air offensive still cherished by the British Air Staff, had prepared themselves and their subordinates in the light of Sperrle's experience in Spain. It did not occur to them that their success threw hardly any light at all on their ability to conduct an entirely different campaign in altogether different circumstances. As long as the German armies were racing through Western Europe, the Luftwaffe had done extremely well because its role was exactly that for which an outlook and an organisation which stressed the supreme importance of speed, surprise and mobility made it suitable. But speed, surprise and mobility had hardly anything to do with the problem of smashing the Royal Air Force and the British aircraft industry by methodically attacking objectives whose value must be at least as apparent to Britons as to Germans, and which the British would therefore take care to guard to the utmost capacity of an unsurpassed defensive system. To put the issue with brutal frankness, the Luftwaffe had proved its skill in attacking objectives designated by the army in accordance with the army's needs. The question now to be answered was how it would perform when it relied solely on its own leaders to choose its targets and frame its strategy.

5

The Preliminary Bout

ONE OF THE POINTS made in the memorandum which Jodl put forward to Hitler at the end of June was that all-out air attacks on the United Kingdom, with no holds barred, were not only an indispensable prelude to invasion but offered the best chance of reducing the affair to an unopposed landing or even making it unnecessary for troops to go ashore at all. If the Royal Air Force and its supporting industries could be smashed, wrote Jodl, then Britain would have lost her last weapon, for the Royal Navy would be powerless to injure Germany without air support. At the same time, attacks on ports and shipping must not be relaxed. On the contrary, the Luftwaffe must do all it could to hasten surrender by redoubling its efforts to interrupt supplies.

By early July Luftflotten 2 and 3, having finished with France, were more or less ready to begin on Britain as soon as Göring gave the word. Some units had been sent to Germany to re-equip; but even they were back in the line about the middle of the month. It was for Göring to say how long he needed to put the final touches to his plan, and for him and the Supreme Command to decide in consultation when the battle should begin.

In the end their decision was governed largely—but not wholly—by the state of naval preparations. As it was soon clear that these could not be completed for many weeks, and as Göring believed that he could smash the Royal Air Force in a month, there seemed little point in beginning the all-out air offensive before late July or early August. In accordance with Jodl's theory, Luftflotten 2 and 3 filled in the interval by launching a new series of attacks on ports and shipping, with the emphasis on shipping. Apart from Jodl's theory, there seemed to the leaders of the Luftwaffe a good chance that these operations would help the main assault by forcing the

British to use up their fighters prematurely in order to protect their convoys.

Attacks on ports and shipping were no novelty. The Luftwaffe had been making them since 1939, beginning with raids on the Firth of Forth and Scapa Flow and continuing with an organised offensive against seaborne trade which cost them fifty aircraft in the first five months of war. All that was new was that the tempo was increased and that special roles were assigned to the two Luftflotten in France and the Low Countries.

The Royal Air Force had suffered heavily in the Battle of France, and had every reason to go carefully until the big moment came. The fighter force alone had lost more than four hundred aircraft in three weeks; at Dunkirk it was already scraping the bottom of the barrel. As things turned out, a tremendous spurt by the aircraft industry, lashed forward by the formidable insistence of the new Minister of Aircraft Production, Lord Beaverbrook, that nothing must hamper output of the vital Hurricanes and Spitfires, just enabled Dowding to turn the corner so far as aircraft were concerned; but, even then, he was still two hundred short of his establishment of pilots.

By the time the stepping up of the German offensive against shipping became apparent, Dowding's squadrons, although still inadequately backed by stored reserves, were thus able to seize chances of engaging the enemy in more favourable conditions than had faced them across the Channel. Their response to Kesselring's and Sperrle's efforts brought on the preliminary phase of the Battle of Britain, which lasted, according to the British reckoning, from July 10 to August 12, or, from the German point of view, from July 3 to August 11.

Soon after midday on July 10 a Channel convoy, westward bound, was steaming south-west through the Straits of Dover, almost within spy-glass range of the command post recently set up near Wissant to co-ordinate Kesselring's anti-shipping operations.* Six Hurricanes from the Biggin Hill sector had been ordered to escort it as it passed through the narrowest part of the Straits immediately opposite the sector front. The arrival of the Germans on the Channel coast, and

---

* All times are given in British Summer Time, which remained in force throughout the battle and was retained into the winter.

the success of the German U-boat offensive in June, had made it necessary to reroute practically all ocean traffic to west coast ports within the last few days; but local convoys were still a vital cog in the machinery of distribution, and this was one of them. Coal and coke, in particular, could not have been distributed fast enough to keep the factories at work if coastal traffic had been halted.

As the head of the convoy came abreast of Dover a little before half-past one, neighbouring R.D.F. stations reported that aircraft were mustering behind Calais, and plots began to cluster on the operations tables of No. 11 Group and its sector stations, as well as at Command Headquarters.

In April Air Vice-Marshal Park had left his job at Stanmore to take command of No. 11 Group, with full tactical responsibility for the air defence of London and its approaches from Southwold to Lyme Bay. He took with him to Uxbridge an intimate acquaintance with the Fighter Command system and its workings. He also took the knowledge that the fighter force was none too strong, that two-fifths of it were in his hands, and that too reckless a use of his resources might lose the war in a few hours. A born fighter whose impulse was always to go in and win, he knew that he must curb his pugnacity and 'box clever'.

The first fighters ordered up in response to the R.D.F. warning were a flight of Hurricanes of No. 56 Squadron which had flown south from North Weald that morning and were in readiness at Manston, near Ramsgate. The six pilots were still climbing when the sector controller warned them that the convoy was already being bombed. A few moments later they saw the German bombers and fighters stepped up in three tiers which seemed to soar into the sky like the Eiffel Tower. The bottom layer consisted of about twenty Dornier 17 long-range bombers; above them were a Gruppe of long-range Messerschmitt 110s as close escort with, higher still, a top guard of about twenty short-range Messerschmitt 109s.

The 110s set the pattern for future actions by forming a defensive circle for their own protection and leaving the real work to the 109s. Even so, the new arrivals were hideously outnumbered by the 109s alone. Hardly expecting to come out of the affair alive but nevertheless hoping for a miracle, they achieved one. Three of the six attacked the bombers while the other three engaged the 110s; all six then shook off a counter-attack by the 109s and returned, exhilarated by success, to Manston, where five of them landed in good order and the sixth crash-landed without serious injury to the pilot. In half an hour, after flights or sections from four of Park's squadrons had come and gone, the action was over, the Germans had departed leaving at least three of their aircraft in the Channel, and the German reconnaissance pilot who first spotted the convoy was preparing to celebrate the sinking of one small ship by opening a bottle of champagne. As often happened, both sides believed that they had won.

Nevertheless, at least one rather disturbing fact emerged from the teleprinted reports which reached Stanmore that evening from the fighter groups. When all the figures were added up, it was found that, although the comparatively minor action off Dover was easily the biggest fought that day, the command had flown more than six hundred sorties between dawn and dusk—about twice its daily average over Dunkirk during the withdrawal. This was a big effort for a force trying to husband its forces for the major battle that was expected almost daily, and it underlined the cost in flying time, and consequent wear and tear, of meeting the Admiralty's demand that fighter escort should be provided for the mass of shipping always somewhere off the long stretch of coastline open to attack.

The story was much the same on the next two days. Skirmishes with German anti-shipping forces brought good results in terms of casualties suffered and inflicted; but the average daily effort remained alarmingly high for a quiet period which brought no big attacks on vital targets. Sorties which led to successful actions like that off Dover on the 10th could be afforded: the trouble was that too much was going into routine patrols which led to nothing. The whole point of an early-warning system was that it enabled a commander to guard important targets such as London and the aircraft factories without wearing out his squadrons by flying standing patrols. Yet Dowding, with the finest early-warning system in the world, was in the absurd position of having to do that very thing for the benefit, not of London or the aircraft industry, but of relatively unimportant targets which no one had thought of asking him to protect when he drew up his plans. It was only about a month before the outbreak of war that the danger to coastwise traffic had come to the fore and that the Air Ministry had saddled him with an unforeseen burden by deciding to give him four so-called trade-protection squadrons which he had since received and handed over to Coastal Command.

The stepping up of the German air offensive against shipping brought the problem to a focus, but it was already very much in Dowding's mind. He had warned the Air Ministry that full protection for shipping between the Humber and Land's End would lock up two-thirds of his entire force, and that he might have to stop escorting convoys altogether as soon as heavy attacks began on inland targets. Up to a point, the Air Ministry were not unsympathetic. Their suggestion, made on July 29 after many more convoys and several ports had been attacked, that Dowding should make more use of forward bases near the coast, was not very helpful, since the bases were already taking all the traffic they could safely bear; yet at least it showed that the Air Staff understood that the ideal solution was to make interception so timely and certain that standing escort would no longer be demanded. But the ideal was never attained. At the height of the Battle of the Atlantic Dowding's successor and *ex-officio* critic, Sir William Sholto Douglas, found it necessary to provide standing escort for shipping on a prodigious scale—an expedient open to him only because he had many more squadrons than Dowding and did not have to beat off massive attacks in daylight to save the country from being knocked out of the war.

The problem had something in common with one which Dowding had come up against at a much earlier stage of his career. In 1916, as commander of the headquarters wing under Trenchard at the Battle of the Somme, he had chafed at his chief's insistence on his flying continuous—and therefore weak—patrols instead of saving up his strength so that he could do something worth while when his contribution was really needed. In those days he was powerless to reverse a policy which cost the flying corps far more casualties than it inflicted; and even a mild request that he should be allowed to rest one squadron led to his being sent home with a black mark against his name.

This time events shelved the question without a showdown between Dowding and the Admiralty or the Air Ministry. The demand for standing escort for Channel convoys was not formally withdrawn until the end of August; but well before that time it was obvious that the fighter force was fighting everybody's battle and must be given a free hand. In the meantime Dowding did his best

19 *Air Vice-Marshal T. L. Leigh-Mallory,*
No. 12 Group

20 *Air Vice-Marshal K. R. Park,*
No. 11 Group

21 *Air Vice-Marshal R. E. Saul,*
No. 13 Group

22 *Air Vice-Marshal Sir*
Quintin Brand, No. 10 Group

BRITISH GROUP COMMANDERS

to compromise between compliance with the Admiralty's demands and avoidance of the 'final, complete and irremediable defeat' which he might have suffered in the next stage of the battle if he had gone too far to meet their wishes.

Meanwhile Luftflotte 2 kept up the offensive, attacking two convoys off Harwich on July 13 and one off Dover on the 14th; Luftflotte 3 had already attacked warships at Portsmouth and Portland and bombs had fallen on the naval dockyard at Portsmouth and elsewhere on shore. The air fighting went strongly in Fighter Command's favour for the first nine days, the Germans losing sixty-one aircraft to Dowding's twenty-eight. But there was a sharp change on July 19, when No. 141 Squadron, one of Dowding's highly-vulnerable Defiant squadrons, took a terrible battering off Dover and lost six of the nine aircraft with which it went into action. That day Fighter Command lost eight aircraft and the Germans only two.

After two more days of give-and-take indifferent weather brought a respite on the 22nd and 23rd. At nightfall on the 23rd the score stood at eighty-five to forty-five in Dowding's favour; but the real question was not so much whether Dowding could give better than he got as whether he could escape losses which might cripple him on the eve of the main assault. The newspapers exulted at the pasting the Germans were getting in the Channel, but Dowding knew that the enemy had used only a fraction of his strength and that the real test was still to come.

On July 24 Kesselring teased Park with simultaneous attacks on convoys in the Thames Estuary and the Straits. Anxious lest a follow-up should catch sectors with too few aircraft at readiness to meet it, the group responded cautiously, and it seemed a miracle, when results were totted up that evening, that they were still in Fighter Command's favour even though Park's forces on the spot had been heavily outnumbered in the fiercest combats of the day. It was galling for Park, whose instinct was always to sweep the Germans from the sky and damn the consequences, to know that many people must be thinking him too sparing of his numbers; but the policy of keeping something in reserve was the right one, and that had to be his consolation. As often as not there was no telling which of several raids displayed on operations tables was the one that mattered, nor could anyone know when the big blow was coming.

The next day was a bad one for the British although, once more, the air fighting went in their favour. A convoy of twenty-one merchant ships, mostly colliers, which left Southend in the forenoon, escorted by two armed trawlers and six Hurricanes, was shadowed from the start by a German reconnaissance aircraft. As the ships drew abreast of Deal the R.D.F. stations picked up a German formation in the offing, and No. 11 Group sent five Spitfires of No. 54 Squadron from the Hornchurch sector to patrol Dover. Soon afterwards a first wave of about thirty dive-bombers, escorted by Messerschmitt 109s, led off a series of deadly attacks on the convoy. A survivor, Donald Connacher, second mate of the collier *Henry Moon*, at the tail of the convoy, described the Stukas afterwards as looking like 'a flock of rooks with black, crooked wings'.*

The slow-moving, vulnerable Junkers 87 was a difficult aircraft to escort, and the Messerschmitt 109s were too fast to have done the job effectively had Park been able to spare enough aircraft to go all out against both fighters and dive-bombers. As it was, No. 54 Squadron's Spitfires were heavily outnumbered, and the Hurricanes of No. 111 Squadron, sent up from a forward aerodrome at Hawkinge to join them, gained nothing from starting so near the scene of action, for they needed just as long to reach the required height as if they had taken off from their usual base at Croydon, and were handicapped by having to make their climb in full view of the enemy waiting above to pounce on them at a moment of his choosing. Their commanding officer's remark that 'you never had time to gain height before you were attacked' was an apt comment on the Air Ministry's implied rebuke to Dowding for not making greater use of forward aerodromes.

Even so, the dive-bombers suffered fairly heavily; but they were numerous and their aim was good. While they and the long-range bombers which followed them were sinking five ships and crippling another six, the Germans were preparing to finish off the convoy by sending out E-boats in broad daylight. Vice-Admiral Sir Bertram Ramsay, commanding at Dover, responded by ordering out two destroyers, which broke up the E-boat flotilla but then came under fire from shore batteries and were recalled. On the way home they were attacked by the better part of a Gruppe of dive-bombers and one of them was damaged. Under cover of darkness

* Alexander McKee, *Strike from the Sky*, 1960.

more E-boats crept out from the French coast and sank three of the crippled ships.

With almost half the convoy gone, the Admiralty decided that the pace had become too hot, and suspended sailings of merchant shipping through the Straits while they worked out new arrangements for passing convoys through the most dangerous areas at night and escorting them more effectively by day. The first group of ships to sail under the new dispensation, a relatively unimportant east-bound convoy, left Falmouth on August 5 and reached the Thames Estuary in safety by lying up by day in well-defended harbours. The real test would come when the sun rose on an important west-bound convoy due to leave the Thames Estuary on the night of August 7.

In the meantime there were no more Channel convoys for Kesselring and Sperrle to attack and for Park reluctantly to provide with standing escort. In the first week of August the number of sorties flown by Fighter Command fell to a daily average of about four hundred and thirty.

Not content to harry east coast convoys, and warned by Göring that henceforth he would be expected to inflict as much damage as possible on the Royal Navy in preparation for invasion, on July 27 Kesselring played a new card by sinking two destroyers and damaging a third. Next day the Admiralty acknowledged that command of the Straits in daylight had been temporarily lost, and the Dover destroyers were withdrawn to Portsmouth. Sperrle had his turn on the 29th, when yet another destroyer sank after an attack by his anti-shipping force. But minesweepers continued to keep the searched channels open, venturing brazenly where destroyers were now forbidden to show themselves in daylight.

Towards nightfall on August 7 the first west-bound Channel convoy of the new series assembled in the Thames Estuary. Two destroyers with a better anti-aircraft armament than the armed trawlers previously used provided surface escort; additional protection against dive-bombing was given by barrage-balloons flown from specially-modified vessels. At first light, after the ships had rounded the North Foreland and passed through the Straits in darkness, a strong fighter escort would meet them off the south coast.

Unfortunately for this plan, within the last fortnight Luftwaffe technicians had erected on the cliffs at Wissant a radar set capable of detecting shipping (and also aircraft) on the far side of the Straits. This was a fact apparently unknown to the organisers of the convoy, although the British Government had long ago been warned that the Germans had something of the kind.

The result was that the darkness on which the Admiralty relied to see the convoy through the danger-area proved its undoing. The ships were duly detected entering the Straits. Unseen in the night, an E-boat flotilla raced across the Channel, the roar of its engines masked by the familiar drone of a few night bombers, to lie in wait beside the searched channel through which the convoy would have to pass. Lulled by the comfortable belief that at any rate they were tolerably safe till morning, officers and ratings went about their jobs or dossed down for a few hours while their ships were steadily steaming into ambush.

In the small hours of August 8 the head of the convoy sprang the trap, and all hell broke loose. The E-boats harried the ships relentlessly along the Sussex coast, sinking two and damaging a third, and causing such confusion that two ships collided, bringing the total to three sunk and two damaged before morning. By the time Dowding's fighters were due to start escorting the convoy, there was no convoy to escort, but only scattered groups of ships strung out over many miles of sea.

Luckily for the survivors, the very success of the E-boat attack helped many of them to escape disaster. Irretrievably separated from their escort, they would have been easy prey for the Luftwaffe if the Luftwaffe had known where to find them and had not believed that most of them had been sunk already. Probably because of the time needed to sort out reports from E-boat commanders and reconnaissance aircraft, and perhaps also because there must have been some doubt as to whether most of the ships were in Kesselring's area or Sperrle's, Luftflotte 3's first attack was not delivered until several hours had been lost. The Germans tended, too, to go for half a dozen small craft sent from Portsmouth to the rescue, rather than for merchant ships which had fallen far behind their estimated positions and were hard to find. Even so, more than half the twenty-five merchant ships of the original convoy were hit by bombs or E-boat fire, and at least six of them, in addition to the one sunk by collision, were total losses.

The preliminary phase of the battle was now drawing to a close.

On July 30 the Führer had told Göring to be ready to begin the main assault at twelve hours' notice; but Göring, whose plans were not yet complete although he had had a whole month to do the job, had begged a respite. Apparently satisfied that the weather was not going to be good for several days, he then waited a week before telling Luftflotte commanders to begin operations on August 10 in accordance with a directive issued on the 2nd. At last, on August 12, Kesselring and Sperrle wound up the preliminary phase with a series of attacks on aerodromes and radar stations in preparation for the big blow which had been further postponed until the morning of the 13th.

At the end of the preliminary bout, both sides believed that they had won on points. As nearly always happened, each side grossly overestimated the other's losses. When the German records became available in Britain at the end of the war, the figures differed so much from claims made in 1940 that some people wondered whether the records had been faked for purposes of propaganda. The simple answer is that the German records were based on returns which units had to make to get replacements. To understate his losses in such a case is about the last thing any commander would do.

However, the Luftwaffe's belief that it had come off best was not based solely on exaggerated estimates of Dowding's losses. Luftflotten 2 and 3 and the German Naval Staff could point with satisfaction to the convoy actions in the Channel on July 25 and August 8 —both undeniable set-backs for the British even though the number of ships sunk was fewer than the Germans thought. The blow to the Admiralty's plans was an established fact, as was the conspicuous absence of British destroyers in daylight immediately after Kesselring's successes on July 27 and Sperrle's on July 29. Superficially there seemed to be a good deal in the claim that Kesselring and Sperrle, after driving ocean traffic from the Port of London, went on to demonstrate their ability to close the Straits to British shipping.

But sober examination of the facts leaves little of this claim intact. The Admiralty's decision to divert practically all ocean traffic to west coast ports was taken in June, before Kesselring's and Sperrle's offensive against Channel convoys was as much as thought of. When a dive-bomber attack on an outward-bound Atlantic convoy off Portland on July 4 was followed by the cessation of such traffic, it was natural that Sperrle should conclude that he had won an important victory at the very outset, and indeed before the battle was reckoned by the Royal Air Force to have begun. But all he had done, in fact, was to confirm the wisdom of the British decision to stop sending outward-bound ocean convoys by that route, and encourage the Admiralty to make the new arrangements more comprehensive by extending them to homeward-bound convoys already at sea and bringing all ocean traffic in and out of the west coast ports by a single route. In other words, where the ocean convoys were concerned the Luftwaffe's contribution was not so much to close the Port of London to ocean traffic as to make it clear to all concerned that the Admiralty were on the right track when they warned the Government that the traffic would have to be rerouted because the French coast, with its U-boat bases and aerodromes, was falling into German hands.

As for the argument that Kesselring's and Sperrle's achievements proved their ability to close the eastern half of the Channel to British shipping, the facts are that the claim was never made by the German leaders themselves except in the most guarded terms, and that they expressly disclaimed the power to exercise control in darkness. Colonel Fink, commander of Kesselring's anti-shipping force, is reported to have said, significantly, that, *given air superiority*, his bombers and fighters could have dominated the Straits in daylight but not at night, and to have added that, *if the Royal Air Force had been beaten*, the Luftwaffe could have kept British warships from the invasion area, again in daylight only. But Fink was not 'given air superiority', and the Royal Air Force was not beaten. Air superiority remained in dispute throughout the principal phases of the battle, until in the end the Luftwaffe was forced to call off attempts to gain it. The purely local and temporary superiority which Kesselring gained in the preliminary phase was meaningless, since neither side was at full stretch.

Nor did Kesselring's and Sperrle's efforts in the preliminary phase fulfil, to any appreciable degree, the far-reaching aims outlined in Jodl's memorandum. The objects of the air war against Britain, as defined by Jodl, were to undermine the system of food supply, to paralyse and finally break the will of the people to resist, and to smash the Royal Air Force and the industries on which it depended for replacements. None of these objects was achieved. A temporary interruption of Channel convoys, and the loss of thirty thousand tons of shipping out of a million tons which flowed between British ports during the five weeks of the preliminary offensive, did not cause a single Briton to go hungry; and the will of the people to resist was not at all paralysed by the frequent drubbings inflicted by Kesselring's and Sperrle's forces.

As for the third object, the facts are that Luftwaffe units facing the United Kingdom lost close on three hundred aircraft in active operations between July 10 and August 12, but that these losses did not prevent them from having more serviceable aircraft at their disposal two days before the end of the preliminary offensive than they had ten days after it began. During the same period the British lost a hundred and fifty fighters in active operations against the Luftwaffe, and their factories turned out more than five hundred Hurricanes and Spitfires. In other words, the preliminary phase made no practical difference to the relative first-line strength of the two sides, but it left the British with substantially increased numbers of aircraft both with squadrons and in stored reserves.

Since supply was bound to be a crucial factor in the next stage of the battle, this outcome was a striking vindication of Dowding's policy of caution, and a tribute to Park's loyalty and judgment. It was also a victory for the aircraft industry and the much-criticised Lord Beaverbrook, who exceeded the expectations of the Chiefs of Staff by fifty per cent while the battle of the convoys was in progress, thus making it possible for Dowding to win the far more important contest he was now drawing breath to fight.

6

Four Steps to Failure: One and Two

AUGUST 13 and 15

WHEN HITLER ANNOUNCED on July 30 that he expected the Luftwaffe to be ready to launch 'the great air battle of the German Air Force against England' at short notice, Göring had not yet made up his mind how to set about the job. Next day, after weighing conflicting advice from Kesselring and Sperrle, he decided to simulate a major attack on London in order to draw up Dowding's fighters and destroy them in the air.

After a day or two no more was heard of the first part of this intention, but the second part was reflected in orders to operational commanders to keep close escort of bombers to the minimum in order to free as many as possible of the short-range, high-perform-ance fighters for independent sweeps in the target area. This meant that, at any rate in the early stages of the battle while air superiority was being sought, Kesselring's and Sperrle's striking forces would have to be kept down to the numbers which could be escorted by about two hundred long-range fighters and such short-range fighters as could be spared from their freelance role. At the same time Göring, refusing to shake off his allegiance to blockade, decreed that attacks should still be made on commercial ports and harbours. Naval targets also continued to figure in the programme, which included plans for a major attack on Scapa Flow.

Notwithstanding unequivocal instructions from Hitler that the Luftwaffe's attacks were to be 'directed primarily against the flying units, ground organisation and supply installations of the Royal Air Force, and against the air armaments industry', the German offensive was thus bedevilled from the start by the failure of the High Command to bring its aims to a clear focus. Every rule of strategy demanded that the men at the top should direct the minds of commanders in the field unmistakably to the main objective, and leave them to find the right means of attaining it in the light of tactical conditions and the best information the intelligence service could provide. Göring and his headquarters staff did almost the opposite. They sowed confusion by drawing attention to a wide range of objectives, and they intervened in matters of detail whose relevance they were not well placed to assess. Conferences at which Göring lectured Kesselring and Sperrle on their tactical shortcomings were no substitute for a clear and simple directive which did not ask too much, and which left no room for doubt as to whether the purpose of bombing was to destroy targets or bring on a fighter battle.

The attacks made by Kesselring and Sperrle on August 12 as a curtain-raiser to the all-out offensive were aimed at Park's forward aerodromes at Manston, Lympne and Hawkinge; six R.D.F. stations on the south coast; naval installations at Portsmouth and Gosport; and a convoy in the Thames Estuary. Attacks on ships and naval installations had nothing to do with the primary objective, and could be justified in terms of Hitler's directive only as tactical diversions. But there was no point in tactical diversions if the object of the main attack was to lure fighters to the target area.

On the other hand the rest of the programme conformed quite well with the Supreme Command directive. One R.D.F. station, at Ventnor in the Isle of Wight, took such a battering that a gap was blown in the radar chain which was not filled for the best part of a fortnight. Others were damaged more or less severely. The three aerodromes were all fit for use next day, after craters in landing-surfaces had been hurriedly filled in, but damage to hangars and offices was at any rate a minor contribution to the wearing down of the Royal Air Force.

With extraordinarily bad luck from the German point of view, Göring's repeated postponements resulted in his picking for the start of the main offensive a day when the weather could hardly have been more unsuitable. At dawn on August 13, his final choice for the long-heralded *Adler-Tag*, or 'Eagle Day', a thick bank of cloud, in places down to four thousand feet above sea-level, covered most of Kent and a great part of Sussex. A combination of bombing and high-level fighter sweeps would be almost useless in such conditions, for Dowding's squadrons would be able to concentrate

77

on the bombers and their close escort, ignoring the freelance fighters wheeling aimlessly above the clouds in ignorance of what was going on below.

Accordingly the attacks planned for the morning were called off soon after sunrise. By that time a whole Geschwader of Dornier 17 long-range bombers, about eighty strong, had left their aerodromes in Artois with the object of making rendezvous with their close escort over the French coast before flying to Sheppey to bomb an aerodrome at Eastchurch and the naval harbour at Sheerness, where part of the anti-invasion forces of the Nore Command were stationed. Further west, in Luftflotte 3's area, about the same number of Junkers 88s were preparing to attack aerodromes at Odiham and Farnborough while a strongly-escorted Geschwader of dive-bombers trailed their coats off the Hampshire coast.

Sheerness excepted, these targets satisfied the letter of the Supreme Command directive, but no more than the letter. In order to smash the Royal Air Force, the Luftwaffe must obviously begin by smashing Fighter Command, thus gaining the required air superiority. Yet none of the aerodromes chosen for attack was a Fighter Command station. Eastchurch was a Coastal Command station. True, it housed two squadrons nominally classed as fighter squadrons, but both had been lent indefinitely to the command to which the aerodrome belonged. Odiham was a probable base for army support squadrons if the Germans landed; Farnborough, the Germans may have thought, might also be so used. Meanwhile it was the home of the former Royal Aeroplane Factory, renamed the Royal Aircraft Establishment.

Asked after the war why such targets were chosen in preference to fighter stations, and especially sector stations, survivors of striking forces answered that they attacked Bomber, Coastal and Fighter Command stations indiscriminately, partly because they were not sure which was which, partly because all or any of them could be used by fighters. Although given in good faith, this explanation was almost certainly not the right one. The Luftwaffe High Command had a good knowledge of the disposition of Dowding's squadrons and understood the importance of the sector stations. It seems clear that the true explanation of their apparently random choice of targets was that Göring wanted to do too much in too short a time. Notoriously little interested in the invasion plans of the other services because he thought that they would never be put into effect, he believed that, by attacking a wide range of targets, the Luftwaffe could, at one and the same time, not only destroy Dowding's squadrons in the air but cause such havoc on the ground that the country would be brought to the verge of surrender, or beyond it, by the time the German Army was ready to go ashore.

Through a combination of bad staff work, inadequate signals arrangements and poor discipline, the order calling off the morning's attacks did not reach Fink, who was leading Kesselring's bombers, but was duly received by the leader of the escort force, who took his formation back to base after trying vainly to attract Fink's attention. When he found that his escort was not with him, Fink decided none the less to fly to Sheppey, presumably reckoning that the blanket of cloud which hid the English coast would hamper the defences at least as much as it hampered him.

Meanwhile the radar chain had given Park well over half an hour's warning of his approach, and had also picked up Luftflotte 3's bombers and fighters a hundred miles to the west. Put on his guard by the previous day's events, which hinted at a new departure, Park responded with a well-calculated blend of enterprise and caution. On his left he put up a squadron of Spitfires and two squadrons of Hurricanes, dividing them between a convoy in the Thames Estuary and his forward aerodromes at Hawkinge and Manston, both damaged in the previous day's attacks. In addition he put smaller formations over two aerodromes on his extreme flank in Suffolk. On the right he ordered a section of Hurricanes at Tangmere, near Chichester, to patrol their base, ordering the rest of the squadron to patrol a line from Arundel to Petworth. Finally, he ordered a squadron of Hurricanes from Northolt to take up a position over Canterbury, obviously with the intention of switching them either east or west when the need arose. This disposition left him, after he had reinforced his left with a squadron of Spitfires, less one section, from the Kenley sector, and his right with another Tangmere squadron, with about half his Hurricanes and two-thirds of his Spitfires uncommitted—a fairly generous provision for contingencies, but hardly an excessive one in view of the large forces at the enemy's disposal barely half an hour's flying-time from London.

To the west of Park's group Air Vice-Marshal Sir Quintin Brand, commanding No. 10 Group, had recently taken over the Middle

Wallop sector from his neighbour. His response to what he seems, quite rightly, to have judged to be a fairly remote threat to his area was to put a squadron of Hurricanes over the Dorset coast, and later order up another squadron and a half of Hurricanes from Exeter.

A good hour after Fink's force was first detected over France, he broke cloud near Whitstable with the greater part of his Geschwader, bound for Eastchurch. No. 74 Squadron, the Spitfire squadron sent to keep an eye on Manston, were close at hand—almost too close for success. Their leader, Squadron-Leader A. G. ('Sailor') Malan, was a resourceful commander and one of the most successful of Dowding's pilots. His squadron would have made havoc of Fink's unescorted bombers if they had had time and elbow-room for a series of methodical attacks. As it was, the luck was with Fink. Although he had not seen the ground since crossing the coast, and could judge his whereabouts only by dead reckoning, he succeeded in leading his formation out of the clouds so close to the target that the Spitfires had no chance of doing more than tackle some of the nearest Dorniers while the rest were bombing Eastchurch with fair accuracy.

Almost at the same moment the rest of Fink's Geschwader, bound for Sheerness (with Chatham as a possible alternative), ran into the Hurricanes of No. 151 Squadron, patrolling the Thames Estuary convoy and led by Squadron-Leader 'Teddy' Donaldson. Shaken by the encounter, they dropped their bombs well short of the target and dodged back into cloud. A few moments later the Hurricanes of No. 111 Squadron, at first sent to Hawkinge but since directed by the sector controller towards the enemy, came up with part of Fink's force and engaged it. A certain amount of confusion which still surrounds this engagement bears witness to the unfitness of the weather for Göring's plan. Squadron-Leader J. M. Thompson, who led the squadron, was sure that the formation he attacked was the one which bombed Eastchurch, and that he and his pilots watched them do it. A comparison of times and places suggests very strongly that it was really the formation bound for Sheerness and engaged a little earlier by Donaldson.

Meanwhile, a good sixty miles to the west, Sperrle's bombers were crossing the Sussex coast in two formations, both escorted. At exactly the right moment, Park sent in the Hurricanes he had

24 *Spitfires on patrol*

25 *Hurricanes in formation*

26   *British fighter-pilots, 1940*

27   *Refuelling between sorties at Digby*

posted over Canterbury. Arriving in the nick of time, they met one of the German formations near Bognor at almost the same moment as the other was intercepted near Worthing by one of the Tangmere squadrons. Also engaged by the other Tangmere squadron, and by a squadron of Spitfires which doubled back to Sussex after flying towards the Thames Estuary from their base at Kenley, both formations missed their targets. Failing to tempt Park or Brand into action, the eighty-eight strongly-escorted dive-bombers which paraded off the coast returned to France with nothing to show for the wear and tear on their aircraft and their expenditure of time and fuel.

In Luftflotte 3's area the muddle arising from the last-minute attempt at cancellation was not cleared up for several hours. About half-past eleven a Gruppe of Messerschmitt 110s set off from the French coast without the bombers they were meant to accompany. Arriving off Portland about noon, after being continuously tracked across the Channel in spite of the gap blown in the radar chain by the previous day's bombing at Ventnor, they lost five aircraft in combat with two of Brand's squadrons and one of Park's—a performance which gave point to Göring's complaint a day or two later that long-range fighters were being thrown away.

In the afternoon thick clouds down to four thousand to six thousand feet over the Thames Estuary and much of southern England still threatened to make target-finding difficult and gave the Germans a poor chance of bringing on the fighter battle they were seeking. In spite of this handicap Kesselring and Sperrle did their best to redeem the morning's blunders. The plan was that about fifty of Kesselring's bombers, with a strong fighter escort, should attack aerodromes north and south of the Thames Estuary, while about forty of Sperrle's, also well escorted, bombed aerodromes on the edge of Salisbury Plain and dockside buildings at Southampton. It was characteristic of the blindness which afflicted Göring's planners that no one seems to have seen that, as ninety bombers were unlikely to do decisive damage to half a dozen widely dispersed targets, the only point of the operation was the prospect of a fighter battle which was more or less ruled out by the weather.

About half-past three warning was received at No. 10 Group's headquarters at Rudloe that three formations, believed together to be about ninety aircraft strong, were crossing the Channel towards the front of the Middle Wallop sector or slightly to the east of it. Air Vice-Marshal Brand, a distinguished first-war pilot remembered for his part in an epoch-making flight to the Cape, already had a squadron of Spitfires from that sector on patrol near Swanage. Apart from a squadron of Blenheim night-fighters and a flight of obsolescent Gladiators, the rest of his resources consisted of a squadron each of Spitfires and Hurricanes at Middle Wallop, two squadrons of Hurricanes at Exeter and two squadrons of Spitfires far away in Cornwall and South Wales.

Foreseeing that the enemy might take advantage of the weather to slip through the defences, he ordered one of his remaining Middle Wallop squadrons and one from Exeter to patrol Portland above and below cloud, and the last Middle Wallop squadron to take up a position near the Dorset coast. This left him with nothing un-committed within a hundred miles of the probable scene of action except the one squadron still at Exeter; but there was comfort in the airman's adage that a squadron ordered up is, at any rate, safe from destruction on the ground as long as it does not run out of fuel. Later he went still further by putting up one section of the Spitfires far away at Pembrey, in South Wales, and directing it towards the Middle Wallop sector. On his left, No. 11 Group sent a squadron of Hurricanes to patrol the Isle of Wight, and put a section over Tangmere.

If Brand took a risk, the outcome justified it. The first wave of Sperrle's fighters, drawing ahead of the bombers, were met off Portland by one of the Spitfire squadrons from Middle Wallop and the Hurricanes from Exeter. A few minutes later some of the bombers, with more fighters, were intercepted by the Middle Wallop Hurricanes, which took on the fighters but could not prevent the bombers from going on to attack Southampton, where they were hotly engaged by a wide assortment of anti-aircraft weapons but did a fair amount of damage. The other Spitfire squadron from Middle Wallop met more bombers, with their escort well behind them, near the coast, and forced most of them to scatter their bombs widely over the countryside, so that only a few reached their targets. Of the two aerodromes which Sperrle planned to attack, the not very important Andover suffered fairly heavily, while the more valuable Middle Wallop escaped lightly. On the return flight the bombers were further harried by fighters, among them one of

Park's squadrons which was making its second sortie since the morning.

On the other flank, Park had elements from several squadrons on patrol when the first warning was received, and was on the point of adding to them by putting a Spitfire squadron over Dover. Besides doing so, he sent a squadron of Hurricanes from the North Weald sector to the North Foreland, ordered a flight of Spitfires from Kenley towards the coast, and took steps to protect his extreme left at Martlesham. The Spitfires over Dover met the fighter escort of a wave of bombers bound for a Coastal Command aerodrome near Maidstone, but the bombers reached and bombed the target. The rest of Kesselring's bombers, unable to find their targets north of the Thames because of cloud, turned south, were engaged by a Hurricane squadron sent to the North Foreland, and dropped their load at random.

So ended *Adler-Tag*. In spite of the weather, the Luftwaffe had flown a thousand fighter sorties since dawn, their opponents seven hundred. The German bomber effort, a night attack on the Morris works at Castle Bromwich included, amounted to close on five hundred sorties. The big punch on which Göring counted to lure British fighter squadrons to their doom had cost him forty-five aircraft lost against thirteen aircraft (but only seven pilots) lost by Dowding. Beginning with high hopes, the Germans had taken the first step to failure.

They took the second step on August 15, when they carried out the programme intended for the 14th after losing a day because the weather was again unsuitable.

The main feature of the second day's programme was that, for the first time, fairly weighty attacks across the North Sea were to be made by General Stumpff's Luftflotte 5 in concert with further attacks in the south by Kesselring and Sperrle. This was an extremely risky innovation, for Stumpff was in no position to attack well-defended targets. The plan stood or fell by the assumption that the first day's operations must have used up so many of Dowding's fighters that he would have made haste to denude his sectors in the north and Midlands for the benefit of Park and Brand.

But Dowding had done nothing of the kind, and would probably have done nothing of the kind even if his losses on Eagle Day had been as heavy as the Germans thought they were. An awkward customer from Göring's point of view, he was the last man to shuttle his forces backwards and forwards to suit his enemy. His experience at the Somme a quarter of a century earlier had convinced him of the importance of resting overworked or tired pilots, and he made a practice of rotating squadrons between active and quiet sectors. In other respects the disposition of his forces was substantially the same on August 15 as on August 13. It was, in fact, to change very little throughout the battle.

Stumpff may have had his own opinion of the optimistic forecasts of the High Command; but he could scarcely refuse the part assigned to him. His orders were to attack aerodromes near Newcastle and in Yorkshire, and he had roughly sixty-five Heinkel 111s, fifty Junkers 88s and thirty-five Messerschmitt 110s with which to do it. The 110s were far too few to escort a hundred and fifteen bombers, and had barely the endurance to cross the North Sea in both directions. Making the best of a bad job, he fitted them with supplementary fuel-tanks; ordered them to fly without rear-gunners to compensate for the added weight; sent them to Newcastle with the Heinkels; and ordered the faster and more modern Junker 88s to fly to Yorkshire unescorted. It was a desperate gamble, but it might conceivably come off.

The R.D.F. stations on the east coast picked up the Heinkels and their escort when they were still far out to sea. Their first estimate was that more than twenty aircraft were approaching, but later they raised the figure to more than thirty, and finally to more than fifty. The stations said, correctly, that the aircraft were flying in three distinct formations.

Air Vice-Marshal R. E. Saul, commanding No. 13 Group, was less well known to the public than his colleagues to the south, whose forces were in the thick of the fighting throughout the battle. August 15 gave him his first chance of countering a big attack in daylight. In spite of the enormous area he had to cover, he made such good use of it that it also proved to be his last, for the Germans never repeated the experiment.

Saul's position at noon, when the Heinkels of Kampfgeschwader 26 and the Messerschmitt 110s of Zerstörergeschwader 76 were first detected miles away over the North Sea, was that he had three squadrons of Spitfires, one of Hurricanes, and one of Blenheims in the two sectors which covered the north of England. Of the remaining eight squadrons which made up the resources of his group, four and a half were far away in Northern Ireland, Shetland and the north of Scotland. To supplement the five squadrons immediately at hand he could count only on two and a half squadrons of Hurricanes near the Firth of Forth and a squadron of Defiants near the Clyde. The Blenheims were no match for even long-range fighters, while the Defiants had suffered crippling losses in their last encounter with the Germans and were at least a hundred miles from any objective which Stumpff was likely to attack.

Saul began by sending one of the four single-seater squadrons close at hand to meet the enemy well off the coast. At the same time he brought down a squadron of Hurricanes from the Firth of Forth to patrol Tyneside—an almost unprecedented step. As the threat became more imminent he added the remaining three single-seater squadrons immediately available, keeping back only the Blenheims, the Defiants, and a squadron and a half of Hurricanes near the Forth. By this time correctly appreciating that he had the greater part of Stumpff's resources on his front, he nevertheless responded to a call for reinforcement from No. 12 Group, on his southern flank, by parting with the Blenheims, his only uncommitted squadron within reach. Like Brand in face of Sperrle's threat on the 13th, at least he ran little risk of being caught by Stumpff with his aircraft on the ground.

Meanwhile, to seaward of the Farne Islands, the Spitfires of No. 72 Squadron from Acklington were closing with Stumpff's escorted bombers at the rate of something like eight miles a minute. In the absence of a squadron-leader, they were led by Flight-Lieutenant Edward Graham, who thus stepped into the place of honour in one of the most spectacularly successful air combats of the war.

Thirty miles off the coast, the squadron sighted the enemy—a hundred aircraft to their twelve. As the R.D.F. stations had predicted, the Germans were flying in three formations—the bombers ahead and the fighters in two waves stepped up to the rear. Misled by the supplementary fuel tanks slung below the fighters, which looked like bombs, Graham and his pilots took the nearer wave for Junkers 88s.

Stumpff's armada was so vast in comparison with Graham's little force that Graham hesitated for a moment, uncertain at what point and from what direction to attack it. Apparently unable to bear the suspense, one of his pilots asked whether he had seen the enemy. With a slight stutter which was habitual, and which gave point to his answer, he replied that he had. He was just wondering what to do.

He did not hesitate for long. The Spitfires had had plenty of time to gain height during their long flight from the coast, and were about three thousand feet above the enemy's mean height. Making the most of his advantage and of what corresponded to the weather-gauge, he decided to lead the squadron in a diving attack from up-sun, leaving each pilot free to choose his own target. Two-thirds attacked bombers or supposed bombers, the remaining third the second wave of fighters, correctly identified as 110s.

The results were startling. Jettisoning their external tanks, some of the 110s formed the usual defensive circle, while others dived almost to sea-level and were last seen heading east. The bombers, less an indeterminate number destroyed by Graham's squadron, then split into two formations, each accompanied by some of the remaining fighters. One formation headed for Tyneside, apparently with the intention of bombing Saul's sector station at Usworth; the rest turned south-east towards two aerodromes at Linton-upon-Ouse and Dishforth which they had been ordered to attack.

The first formation, engaged successively by the remaining Spitfire squadron from Acklington, the Tyne guns, and some of the Hurricanes which had come south from Scotland, dropped most of their bombs in the sea. The second, engaged by a squadron of Spitfires from Catterick, a Hurricane squadron from Usworth and the Tees guns, dropped theirs almost as ineffectively near Sunderland and Seaham Harbour. From first to last Saul's fighters, backed by the guns of the 7th Anti-Aircraft Division under Major-General R. B. Pargiter, destroyed eight Heinkels and seven 110s without suffering a single casualty.

While these excitements were at their height, the fifty Junkers 88s which made up the rest of Stumpff's bomber force were speeding across the North Sea towards their objective in South Yorkshire, a bomber aerodrome at Great Driffield. About a quarter of an hour before the first shot was fired off the Farne Islands, warning was received in the operations room of No. 12 Group at Watnall that

German aircraft were approaching the front of the group's Church Fenton sector, but were still a long way out to sea. The R.D.F. stations began by putting the enemy's strength at a squadron or less, but afterwards raised their estimate to a minimum of thirty aircraft.

Air Vice-Marshal Trafford Leigh-Mallory, commanding No. 12 Group, was a controversial figure. A spruce, well-turned-out man with a lively mind, he had a trick of thrusting his thumbs into the outside breast-pockets of his tunic. Much liked by his subordinates, he invited unfavourable comment elsewhere by sometimes lending his support to criticisms of his colleagues which were not always fair or well considered. In view of his later association with a school of thought which held that Park used his squadrons too sparingly, an interesting feature of his response to Stumpff's threat on August 15 is that, apart from putting a squadron of Defiants from Kirton-in-Lindsey over a convoy and borrowing a squadron of Blenheims from Saul, he made no use of units outside the sector immediately threatened, although, according to the published order of battle, he had, in other sectors, at least three single-seater squadrons which were not too far off to have been used.*

Fortunately the disposition he did make proved reasonably successful. Of the two single-seater squadrons from Church Fenton on which Mallory relied, the first met the Junkers 88s off Flamborough Head, and one flight of the second engaged them just as they were about to cross the coast. Between them, the dozen Spitfires and half-dozen Hurricanes which went into action accounted for eight of Stumpff's fifty bombers. Even so, about thirty reached and bombed their primary objective, the aerodrome at Great Driffield, while others dropped bombs at Bridlington and elsewhere. Saul's Blenheims chased the survivors for many miles, but were just not fast enough to catch them. In spite of the fairly satisfactory outcome, it is difficult not to feel that Leigh-Mallory, perhaps misled

---

* These were No. 222 Squadron at Kirton-in-Lindsey and Nos. 611 and 46 Squadrons at Digby. The distances (up to seventy miles or more) were great, but not as great as that covered by the Hurricanes of No. 605 Squadron which flew more than eighty miles from Drem, on the Firth of Forth, to fight off Tyneside. There was also a squadron of Blenheims at Digby, but it was in fairly constant use as a night-fighter squadron. The rest of Leigh-Mallory's squadrons were too far south to come into the picture.

To what extent Leigh-Mallory intervened personally in this action is not clear from published accounts. Responsibility is attributed to him in accordance with the principle outlined in the footnote on page 53.

by the smallness of the first R.D.F. estimate, missed a chance of punishing Stumpff's unescorted bombers much more heavily.

Further south, in Nos. 10 and 11 Groups, events did not go so well for the defences. About an hour after the bombing of Great Driffield close on forty well-escorted dive-bombers from Kesselring's command made a successful attack on one of Park's aerodromes in Suffolk without serious interference from the eighty to ninety fighters put up to intercept them. Almost simultaneously some of Kesselring's long-range bombers attacked the Short aircraft factory at Rochester, doing damage which held up production of the eagerly-awaited Stirling bomber; in addition Eastchurch was attacked again, Hawkinge was bombed for the second time since daybreak, and Fighter Command lost nine aircraft in combat to Kesselring's four or five. In the next few hours a naval aerodrome at Worthy Down was slightly damaged, and fighter aerodromes at Middle Wallop, West Malling and Croydon were fairly heavily bombed by crews who believed that they were attacking Andover, Biggin Hill and Kenley; but this time the Germans lost thirty-two aircraft to Dowding's twenty-one.

Yet, on balance, the day spelled failure for Göring. Both sides made their biggest effort yet, the Luftwaffe flying nearly eighteen hundred sorties and Dowding's squadrons close on a thousand. The Germans were never again to fly so many in one day; yet, instead of the series of decisive actions in their favour which they expected, the outcome was the loss of seventy-five of their own aircraft to Dowding's thirty-four. With more Hurricanes and Spitfires ready for immediate issue as replacements than the two hundred he had lost in the past six weeks, and with British factories still turning out ten or more a day, Dowding could afford, if not to smile, at any rate to await without despair what the next few days might bring. He would have been happier if he had not been well short of his establishment of pilots; but the vital Hurricane and Spitfire squadrons still had an average of nineteen each, of whom at least sixteen were reckoned fully trained and fit for active service. So far the Germans had failed to wear him down. The question was whether they could yet deliver the crushing blow that might extinguish in a day or two the dwindling store of men and machines which would otherwise last him many weeks and might just enable him to win.

28 *German aircrew running to their Heinkel 111s*

29 *Hurricanes taking off to intercept the enemy*

30 *Göring in the midst of a group of German airmen*

31 *Hitler talking to Adolf Galland, the fighter ace*

7

Four Steps to Failure: Three and Four

AUGUST 16 and 18

AFTER THE LUFTWAFFE's all-out effort on August 15, the Intelligence Section of the German Air Staff calculated that Dowding had lost five hundred and seventy-four aircraft in combat since the beginning of July, and that losses other than in combat must have brought his gross wastage to a round total of seven hundred and seventy. Estimating input from new production at not more than three hundred aircraft, and crediting him with a first-line strength of nine hundred aircraft at the start of the preliminary phase, they arrived, by a simple process of addition and subtraction, at the conclusion that he could not have more than four hundred and thirty aircraft left, of which three hundred might be serviceable on the morning of August 16.

Except that the estimate of Dowding's strength at the beginning of the preliminary phase was not far out, these calculations were hopelessly at fault. Since early July combat losses had cost the British not five hundred and seventy-four fighters but two hundred and five. The number of Hurricanes, Spitfires and Defiants turned out by British factories since the end of June was nearer seven hundred and fifty than three hundred. Not all these machines were a direct addition to combat strength; some went to squadrons forming, re-equipping or working up, some to the 'Group Pools', or Operational Training Units, which put pilots through the last stage of their training. Nevertheless the true position on the morning of August 16 was that, after all such allocations had been made, the Aircraft Storage Units from which Dowding's wastage was made good from day to day had two hundred and thirty-five Hurricanes and Spitfires ready for immediate issue when he needed them.

Fighter Command had just under fourteen hundred pilots towards an establishment of 1,588 and the forty-seven Hurricane and Spitfire squadrons reckoned fully operational had, between them, more than enough serviceable aircraft to take the air at their normal tactical strength of twelve aircraft each.

At the same time, the outlook for Fighter Command was not quite as rosy as this analysis suggests. Disquieting features of the situation from the British point of view were that well over half Dowding's losses had occurred in the last ten days, so that reserves of Hurricanes and Spitfires, after climbing fairly steadily since Dunkirk, were dwindling; and—what was worse—that trained pilots could not be turned out anything like as fast as aircraft.

The fact remained that, with fewer than seven hundred serviceable short-range fighters in France and the Low Countries, the Luftwaffe had nothing like overwhelming numerical superiority. The German bomber force was still impressively large, in spite of recent losses; but bombers, needing short-range fighters to protect them at close quarters, could be more of a liability than an asset in an all-out fighter battle. Had Dowding been free to concentrate his whole force in the corner of England within reach of the Messerschmitt 109, he would have been able to match Kesselring's and Sperrle's short-range fighters with equal, or even slightly superior, numbers of his own. As things were, he felt bound to disperse his resources fairly widely, not only because the rest of the country could not be left more or less at the mercy of unescorted or weakly escorted bombers, but also because his deepest convictions warned him that the biggest blunder he could make was to leave himself without the means of relieving tired squadrons by bringing in fresh ones from quiet sectors. Thus the true comparison, if it came to an all-out contest between short-range fighters on the one side and the other, would be between the six to seven hundred Messerschmitt 109s which the Germans could muster by throwing in all they had, and the two to three hundred Hurricanes and Spitfires which Park and his colleagues on either flank might be able to put into the air from the nine or ten sectors covering southern England from Wessex to East Anglia.

But even then it did not follow that, measuring fighter against fighter, the Germans would have an effective superiority of two to one or more. Well served by an excellent system of early warning and control, Dowding's squadrons could count on a big advantage over German fighters working near the limit of their radius of action and fettered by the needs of striking forces. Worried by bomber losses, Göring increased the handicap when he ruled on August 15 that a higher proportion of the short-range fighters should stay near the bombers. On one of his visits to units in the field, he stormed at Kesselring's fighter leaders, telling them that they had the finest aircraft in the world, and asking what more they needed to chase the British from the skies. 'I request', the fighter ace Adolf Galland claims to have replied, 'that my unit be re-equipped with Spitfires.' Galland was being intentionally provocative, for in fact he knew of nothing better than the Messerschmitt 109 for the 'free-hunting' patrols on which he would have liked the German fighter force to concentrate. His point was that the 'slower and more manœuvrable' Spitfire might, even so, be a better aircraft for the close-escort work on which his chief insisted.

Like another of Göring's orders, forbidding further attacks on radar stations, which Göring thought a poor investment, the rule that more fighters should be devoted to close escort was not always observed in practice. But the decision ushered in a period of fierce controversy in the Luftwaffe. It marked the beginning of the end of a feeling among German fighter pilots that they were bound to win.

Outwardly, August 16 turned out by no means a bad day for the Germans. In spite of their big effort on the previous day, they managed more than seventeen hundred sorties by day and night. On the 15th Göring had complained, rather oddly in view of his earlier insistence that attacks on ports and naval installations should be kept up, that bombs were being wasted on objectives whose destruction did not directly affect the Royal Air Force. In the light of this criticism Kesselring and Sperrle devoted practically their whole effort on the 16th to aerodromes, the latter disobeying the letter of his instructions only to the extent of condoning a fresh attack on the damaged R.D.F. station at Ventnor.

Kesselring's main contribution was an attack about midday on a fighter station at West Malling by seventy or more long-range bombers with a strong fighter escort. The Hurricanes of No. 111 Squadron, taking off from Hawkinge and led with almost uncanny skill by Squadron-Leader J. M. Thompson, cut across the bows of the bombers and attacked them accurately and effectively from head-on. Rudolf Lamberty, a German bomber pilot who had a good view of the engagement, was much impressed by the performance of the British fighters, which seemed to him to put that of the German escort in the shade. But Thompson and his pilots were too few to prevent the bulk of the bombers from going on to bomb West Malling. As no fighter squadrons were permanently based there at the time, however, the bombing was more of an irritant than a real set-back to Fighter Command's ground organisation.

Further west, Sperrle pushed home concerted attacks on a naval aerodrome at Gosport, a Coastal Command aerodrome at Lee-on-Solent, the Ventnor R.D.F. station and Park's sector station at Tangmere, near Chichester. The attack on Tangmere, which wrecked buildings, cut electricity and water supplies and destroyed or damaged fourteen aircraft on the ground, was one of the most effective yet made on a Fighter Command station, but it did not prevent fighters from taking off and landing. During the attack on Gosport Flight-Lieutenant J. B. Nicholson of No. 249 Squadron from the Middle Wallop sector was badly burned when his Hurricane caught fire, but kept up his attack on a German long-range fighter until he was forced to bale out. In spite of his injuries he managed to pull the rip-cord, but was then shot at by members of the Home Guard who either mistook him for a paratrooper or thought a baled-out German airman fair game. He received the first Victoria Cross awarded to a Fighter Command pilot. To wind up a day which ought, according to programme, to have put the Luftwaffe within sight of victory, Sperrle made a number of other attacks on aerodromes and destroyed forty-six training aircraft on the ground at Brize Norton, on the borders of Oxfordshire and Gloucestershire.

After going all-out for two successive days, the Luftwaffe made no major attacks on August 17, despite tolerably good weather—an omission which throws an interesting light on Hitler's claim in October that only the bad luck which denied his airmen five consecutive fine days robbed him of the chance of landing in England in September. Dowding and the Air Ministry used the respite to take stock of the situation, the former urging that the best pilots from bomber squadrons with obsolete equipment should be drafted into his command, the latter promising to add fifty-three volunteers from such sources to the seventy or eighty new pilots due to complete their training by the end of the month. At the same time they agreed to cut operational training to the minimum needed to give novices some knowledge of the aircraft they would fly on active service. The last was a dangerous expedient, for it meant that new recruits to the fighter squadrons would be more of a liability than an asset until they had picked up a little experience at first hand; but Dowding, with a hundred and fifty pilots killed, wounded or missing in the last ten days and a cumulative deficiency of about two hundred, had no choice but to put up with that disadvantage or see his squadrons grow weaker every day. Admittedly there were people who believed that even the temporary disbandment of some of the less successful squadrons would be better than dilution of the rest by inexperienced newcomers; but that was not a solution which Dowding was ever likely to accept unless it were forced on him.

Soon after midday on the 18th Kesselring launched a fresh series of attacks on two of Park's sector stations, Biggin Hill and Kenley, and two of his other aerodromes, Croydon and West Malling. The plan for the attack on Biggin Hill was that successive high-level attacks, separated by an interval of five minutes, were to be made by two strongly-escorted Gruppen of long-range bombers. Five minutes after the second high-level attack a single squadron of unescorted bombers, flying low to escape detection, was to arrive over the target and administer the *coup de grâce*. Rudolf Lamberty, commanding the single squadron, was told that he would have no difficulty in finding the aerodrome because he would see the smoke and dust raised by the high-level bombing.

Except that the single squadron did escape detection on the way to the target, these arrangements went disastrously wrong. The two high-level formations were duly picked up and plotted in operations rooms. At Biggin Hill the sector commander, Group-Captain R. Grice, watched the plots creeping across the map towards his station, and waited impatiently for orders from Uxbridge to put up his squadron of Spitfires and two squadrons of Hurricanes. Knowing no more of the existence of a low-level formation than the group controller did, but fearing that the high-level formations would reach him before they could be intercepted, he finally took the law into his own hands and did the right thing for more or less the wrong reason by ordering the three squadrons off the ground on his own responsibility.

Punctual to the minute, Lamberty's squadron crossed the Sussex coast at Cuckmere Haven and roared inland over Ashdown Forest and East Grinstead. The ground raced away below the bombers at a speed which Lamberty would have found exhilarating if he had been quite sure that he was not going to miss the target and land in trouble. He had hardly had time to wonder why there was no column of dust and smoke ahead of him when an aerodrome which could only be Biggin Hill flashed up under his bows, undamaged and with its local anti-aircraft defences intact and keyed up to expect the high-level formations.

In addition to light anti-aircraft guns and anti-aircraft guns, the defences included a number of so-called parachute-and-cable sets, consisting of crudely-made projectors firing rockets to which were attached light steel cables buoyed up by tiny parachutes. The effect from Lamberty's point of view was that the air was suddenly filled with what he afterwards described as 'a damn carpet of some kind of rockets'. The squadron only just had time to drop its bombs before Lambert's aircraft collided with one of these cables. Surviving the impact, and climbing steeply in the hope of avoiding further surprises, he ran into a burst of light anti-aircraft fire, was attacked by some of the fighters which had taken off a few minutes earlier, and crash-landed amidst a hail of bullets loosed off by a detachment of the Home Guard. A few minutes after being taken prisoner he narrowly escaped being killed by bombs dropped by high-level bombers which had failed to make punctual rendezvous with their escort and were twenty minutes late. Of the nine aircraft of his squadron which had started, only two landed back at base, one carrying a dead pilot.

The attack on Kenley, six and a half miles to the west, was much more successful. Six Hurricanes were destroyed on the ground, many buildings were wrecked, and a chance hit put the operations room out of action, with the result that one of the three squadrons based at the station had to be withdrawn because the standby operations room could not handle more than two. West Malling and Croydon, already damaged, were again in trouble.

A few hours later Sperrle made one of the multiple raids in which he specialised, attacking aerodromes at Thorney Island, Ford and Gosport, and putting an R.D.F. station at Poling out of action for ten days or more. But German hopes that Dowding's squadrons in the south were near exhaustion were dashed that evening, when bombers and long-range fighters of Luftflotte 2 met fierce opposition over the Thames Estuary. Bound for Park's sector station at North Weald on the north bank of the river, they were engaged near Harwich by Spitfires of No. 54 Squadron from Hornchurch and afterwards by two Hurricane squadrons from the target sector. Savagely punished well short of their objective, they accomplished nothing but some rather aimless machine-gunning of the much-battered Manston on the return journey. With seventy-one aircraft lost since morning—the largest number destroyed in a single day except on the memorable occasion when Stumpff's weakly-escorted bombers made their fatal contribution—the Luftwaffe could not pretend that they had won the air superiority they were seeking.

When the sun went down on August 18, it went down on Göring's chances of doing everything he had set out to do. He had shot his bolt and had failed conspicuously to score. The outcome of the four days which were to have taken him more than half-way to success was that Dowding's squadrons, although hard pressed, were still intact; that there were still a hundred and sixty-one Hurricanes and Spitfires immediately available in stored reserves; that the Luftwaffe had lost two hundred and thirty-six aircraft to Fighter Command's ninety-five; above all, that the confidence of Luftwaffe flying units in the High Command had turned to scepticism. How could the Luftwaffe defeat an enemy who turned up in strength to administer, with apparent unconcern, a crushing blow at the very moment when everyone had just said that he was beaten?

8

The Second Round

WHEN HITLER TOLD GÖRING to begin the great air battle against England, he added that within a fortnight of the start he would decide, in the light of its results, whether invasion should be tried.

Göring's position at nightfall on August 18 was that he had made the four-day effort which was to have brought him air superiority over southern England, and had failed to achieve it. On the other hand, the fortnight was not yet up; nor had he yet been able to deliver all-out attacks on four successive days.

At a conference with his senior commanders on August 19, Göring decided to make another attempt as soon as the weather was suitable, and this time not to overlook the importance of smashing Fighter Command first. He ordered that objectives should be carefully chosen with that end in view; that every available short-range fighter should be brought in to second the efforts of Kesselring's bombers over south-eastern England; and that Kesselring and Sperrle should keep up the pressure all round the clock by sending solitary bombers to attack aircraft factories or air force installations at night or when the weather was unsuitable for all-out attacks by day. Stumpff, stripped of his long-range fighters to console Sperrle for the transfer of most of his Messerschmitt 109s to Kesselring, was to prepare for a night attack on Glasgow; Sperrle for a similar attack on Liverpool. Neither Liverpool nor Glasgow was, however, to be made the object of a major attack except on Göring's express orders.

On the same day, Park summed up some of the lessons of the recent fighting in one of his periodical instructions to sector commanders and controllers. Believing that he was reasonably sure of success if he could only save his sector stations from destruction, inflict steady losses and, at the same time, resist the temptation to swop fighter for fighter with the enemy, he stressed the importance

32 *A German rear-gunner*

33   *Bombing-up Stuka dive-bombers*

34   *A hurriedly snatched meal between sorties*

ON A GERMAN AIRFIELD

of meeting the Germans forward of their objectives and shooting down their bombers.

The argument that Park ought, on the contrary, to have thought first of destroying fighters, because the Germans had more bombers than they could escort and support, is only superficially attractive. Paradoxically, shooting down bombers—if Park could do it—was the best way of defeating not only the enemy's bomber force but also his fighter force, because it would drive Kesselring to lock up more and more of his Messerschmitt 109s in a close escort role for which they were not suited. The less effective they proved to be in that capacity, the louder would grow the demand for them from bomber units, and the more remote Kesselring's chance of gaining a decisive success by throwing in an overwhelming mass of short-range fighters unfettered by the tactical requirements of striking forces. Nothing, therefore, could have been sounder than Park's decision to maintain the efficiency of his force by preserving its vital bases and nerve-centres, go for the enemy's bombers, and avoid being drawn into the all-out fighter-to-fighter action which Kesselring was trying to provoke. Failure to understand this lay at the root of most of the criticisms of Park which were voiced by Leigh-Mallory and others.

The weather was indifferent on August 19, and remained so for the next four days. On the 24th, with only three days to go before the fortnight expired, Göring was at last able to launch his second bid for air superiority. On the credit side of the account, his plans were more intelligently framed than those with which he began the battle. On the debit side, German fighter pilots were learning to distrust the optimism of the High Command, and did not believe that they could win a fighter battle by sticking close to bombers as Göring wanted them to do.

On the morning of the first day of the new phase Kesselring had more than a thousand long-range bombers and short-range fighters fit for active service, Park an effective fighting strength of about two hundred Hurricanes and Spitfires, with the addition of such help as he could reasonably ask from the flanking sectors in Nos. 10 and 12 Groups. The proportion of bombers to fighters in Kesselring's command was such that he could not hope to send more than three hundred bombers across the Channel at one time; but his superior overall strength did enable him to keep his opponent guessing by nearly always having a few machines in the air on his own side of the Straits. The R.D.F. stations could not tell Park which of the aircraft they detected over the French coast were bombers and which fighters; nor was there any means of knowing when a formation in the offing might cross the Channel to attack some vital objective. To some extent Park was therefore forced to match his rival's extravagance, and devote part of his strength to purely precautionary patrols. Besides causing wear and tear to aircraft, these entailed the risk that pilots might be getting tired, or running out of fuel, just when they were needed.

This did, in fact, happen about half-past twelve on the first day of the new phase, after Park's squadrons had been kept busy all the morning without seeing much of the enemy. At a moment when the Defiants of No. 264 Squadron, recently brought south from No. 12 Group, were patrolling Manston and were about to be relieved, one of five German formations detected over the French coast dashed across the Straits, reached Manston without interference and delivered a disconcertingly swift and accurate attack. Nine of the Defiants, refuelling while the other three kept guard above, just managed to get into the air before the bombs fell; but the squadron lost three aircraft in the fight that followed, and Manston was so badly damaged that it had to be abandoned as a permanent base for fighters. The Germans lost five bombers and two fighters in combat with the Defiants and a squadron of Hurricanes on their way to Hawkinge, but could claim to have punched a sizeable hole in the outer crust of Park's defences.

Three hours later Park had five squadrons on patrol when Kesselring sent a substantial force across the Straits to bomb Manston for the second time and also attack the more important Hornchurch and North Weald; but one of the five was just about to land, and two of the others had used up a good deal of their fuel. At Hornchurch the unfortunate No. 264 Squadron were again caught short, this time with seven of their aircraft on the ground when the enemy arrived; but they managed to get into the air while the bombs were falling, and lost another Defiant in their second combat of the day. The station was saved from serious damage largely by its gun defences, which put up such an effective fire that most of the bombers missed the target. At North Weald seven Hurricanes of No. 151 Squadron, led by the station commander,

Wing-Commander Victor Beamish—an Irishman of legendary toughness who had worked as a lumberjack in Canada between spells as a regular air force officer—just got off the ground in time to escape a damaging attack. Once airborne, they engaged the enemy, but found the bombers so well guarded by Messerschmitt 109s that they could not reach them. The fact remains that the force which attacked North Weald, engaged by the Hurricanes of No. 56 Squadron from the neighbouring Rochford as well as by No. 151 Squadron, and also by anti-aircraft guns, lost five bombers and four fighters, against eight British aircraft destroyed and three pilots killed or wounded. Of the five squadrons originally on patrol, at least three engaged German formations on the way to their targets; but they, too, reported that the bombers were hard to reach.

In No. 10 Group Brand's fighters also found that bombers accompanied by a close escort, a top cover, and possibly yet another layer of fighters on freelance patrol above, were difficult to get at. Still able to scrape up enough short-range fighters to send a well-protected force of more than fifty bombers to Portsmouth, while Kesselring was attacking Hornchurch and North Weald, Sperrle had nearly everything his own way. Two and a half squadrons of Brand's fighters, and one and a half of Park's, were airborne near the Isle of Wight when his force approached, but only one squadron were able to get to grips with it before it crossed the coast, and they found themselves in no position to do much. The bombers and their escort were heavily engaged by anti-aircraft fire over the target, but the chief effect was to cause many of them to drop their bombs on the town instead of concentrating on the dockyard, with the result that civilian casualties were exceptionally heavy. All told, the day's events cost Dowding more than twenty aircraft—and that was far too many, even though German losses were nearer forty.

That night the German commanders did their best to give effect to Göring's demand for a round-the-clock offensive by sending a hundred and seventy bombers to attack air force installations and industrial targets not only in south-east England but as far afield as Cardiff, Swansea and South Shields. About a dozen crews were ordered to bomb aircraft factories at Rochester and Kingston and oil refineries at Thames Haven. In spite of an express ban on the bombing of London without specific orders from the High Command, bombs were scattered on the City of London and at least nine other London districts or boroughs by crews who had only the vaguest notion of their whereabouts. A disaster for both sides, this piece of carelessness led the British Government to order the bombing of Berlin on the following night, thus giving Hitler a pretext for the merciless bombing of British cities later in the year and touching off a chain of reactions whose end-product was seen in 1945 at Hiroshima.

Dowding was in no position to shoot down more than an occasional German aircraft at night. This was not because he had no answer to the night-bomber, but because, through no particular fault of his, the answer was not ready. Development and production of the special forms of radar needed by night-fighters and anti-aircraft guns engaging unseen targets had been put second to the needs of the early-warning system. As it happened, Dowding was rather specially interested in the application of radar to night-fighting, but he did not dissent from the argument that the early-warning system must come first because everything depended on it, at night as well as by day, and because a successful German daylight offensive could be decisive. At the same time it was obvious that the beginning of heavy night attacks on the United Kingdom would bring correspondingly heavy pressure on him to produce a remedy which he had no means of producing until the equipment he needed came forward in substantial quantities and was working properly.

Of the hundred and seventy bombers sent over the country between nightfall on August 24 and dawn on August 25, the Germans lost two to the defences—one shot down by a Hurricane of No. 615 Squadron, the other probably by anti-aircraft fire. It was characteristic of Dowding that he did not try to persuade himself or others that this meant that the Germans would soon be losing their night-bombers in substantial numbers. On the contrary, he took an early opportunity of reminding the Air Ministry that the use of Hurricanes at night, without special equipment, could lead to nothing more than 'an occasional fortunate encounter'.

The chief event in daylight on the 25th was an attack by Luft-flotte 3 on Brand's forward aerodrome at Warmwell, in the Middle Wallop sector. In the light of Park's experiences on the previous day at Hornchurch and North Weald, he and Brand put up practically every available fighter in the Tangmere, Middle Wallop and Filton sectors in order to avoid losing aircraft on the ground. Three squadrons met Sperrle's force before it reached the target, but found his forty-five bombers escorted and supported by more than two hundred fighters, and almost impossible to reach. After the bombing, which put the station more or less out of action for eighteen hours, several more squadrons tried to engage the bombers, with similar results. Between them, guns and fighters destroyed twelve German aircraft; but only one of them was a bomber, and the loss of eleven British fighters, and eight pilots killed or wounded, proved the toughness of the combats. At the same time the German fighter losses showed that there was something in the argument of Göring's fighter pilots that they were being sacrificed for the benefit of the bombers—an illogical outcome if one of the main objects of the bombing was to create favourable conditions for a fighter battle.

On the 26th, after a night of scattered bombing, the story of the 24th and 25th was repeated with variations. On No. 11 Group's left, Park's fighters intercepted formations of bombers and fighters bound for his three sector stations north of the Thames Estuary, saving Hornchurch and North Weald; but the two squadrons which took on the force bound for the third station could get nowhere near the bombers, and a squadron which Park had asked Leigh-Mallory to send from Duxford expressly to guard Debden did not so much as see the enemy. The station was badly damaged, and relations between Nos. 11 and 12 Groups were not improved by a dispute as to whether Park had asked for reinforcement too late or Leigh-Mallory had been too slow. On the other flank, three of Park's squadrons and the guns of the 5th Anti-Aircraft Division, under Major-General R. H. Allen, successively engaged a big formation of Sperrle's bombers and fighters and broke it up, with the result that a substantial bomb-load intended for Portsmouth dockyard fell partly in the sea and partly on the outskirts of the town. For the first time since the beginning of the new phase the German bomber force suffered fairly heavily, losing nineteen aircraft throughout the day as compared with twenty-six German fighters lost and thirty-one of Dowding's. These figures brought the cumulative totals for the three days to ninety-nine German and sixty-nine British aircraft lost by day and night.

According to the original time-table, the date had now been reached by which Hitler was to have decided whether the progress of the air offensive justified his going on with his invasion plans.

After an unsatisfactory beginning, results had been so good in the last three days that he did not give up hope that the air war might yet produce the 'specially favourable initial situation' which now seemed to him essential if troops were to go ashore.

On the 27th—the day after a final attempt by Brauchitsch to shake the Führer's verdict that the army's invasion plans must conform with the realities of the naval situation—the Luftwaffe took a rest, although the weather south of the Midlands was fairly good. Next day, with Hitler still in two minds as to his best course, they resumed the offensive with high hopes. In the morning about twenty bombers and their escort bound for Eastchurch were intercepted over Kent by four squadrons, but pushed on to the target, shooting down eight of Park's fighters and damaging at least another four for the loss of five of their own aircraft. About three hours later a similar force on its way to Rochford was also intercepted by several squadrons, among them No. 1 Squadron, who managed to head some of the bombers from the target. Finally, in the afternoon several waves of German fighters swept over east Kent at heights in the neighbourhood of twenty-five thousand feet. They were engaged by a total of seven of Park's squadrons, which destroyed nine aircraft and lost about as many. It was practically impossible for Park and his subordinates to know in advance—except perhaps by inference from the reported height and speed of the incoming formations—that there were no bombers with the German fighters. The fact remains that this was precisely the kind of engagement which best suited Göring's book.

On the 29th the commander of Kesselring's fighter organisation, General Kurt von Döring, claimed that 'unlimited fighter superiority' had been attained. Not entirely convinced but still hopeful, Hitler told Jodl on the following day that he would postpone his decision until September 10 or thereabouts. If he gave the provisional order for invasion on the 10th, and did not afterwards withdraw it, the invasion fleet would sail on September 20 and the troops would land in England on the 21st.

Meanwhile Sperrle had completed his plans to attack Liverpool at night, and Göring had given his approval. Towards dusk on August 28 the first of a hundred and sixty long-range bombers, despatched at two-minute intervals so as to keep the defenders busy as long as possible, left the French coast with orders to make the seven-hundred-mile flight to Merseyside and back. The programme was repeated on each of the next three nights, the number of aircraft despatched ranging from a hundred and seventy-six on the second night to a hundred and forty-five on the last.

The results fell so far short of Sperrle's expectations that, except on the last night, the defenders did not even know what he was trying to do. Hundreds of crews got nowhere near the Mersey and dropped their bombs between the Severn and the Dee, or even further afield, although only a quarter of the six hundred odd who returned to their bases on the four nights admitted that they had failed to reach the target. After the first night's bombing the civil defence authorities reported that bombs had been scattered over an enormously wide area but that the chief target seemed to have been the Midlands. On the second night, when a handful of Stumpff's bombers confused the issue by attacking Tyneside and the Hartle-pools, Liverpool came fourth in a list of five areas which seemed to have been the enemy's main objectives, and the Ministry of Home Security added that no serious damage had been done to any of them. Only on the last night was substantial damage done at Liverpool and Birkenhead, and even then the docks were practically undamaged.

There were no aircraft factories or air force installations of major importance near the Mersey, apart from a maintenance unit at Sealand which had been the target for a 'cloud-hopping' raid by a single bomber in daylight on August 14. The attacks on Liverpool, as Göring's instructions to Sperrle showed, were a departure from the new rule that night attacks should contribute directly to the offensive against the air force and the aircraft industry. As a reversion to blockade they were a dismal failure; they made no difference to the handling capacity of the port or the railways that served it, and so did nothing to interfere with distribution or supply, apart from causing a good deal of suffering and inconvenience which may conceivably have had some effect on production. On the other hand the raids were cheap, costing the Germans only seven bombers lost on the four nights. Perhaps their most important effect was to show up the shortcomings of the night defences, thus giving a handle to Dowding's critics who complained of his inability to find a stop-gap solution to the problem of the night bomber.

9

Eight Days of Crisis

AUGUST 30—SEPTEMBER 6

'THE BATTLE OF FRANCE', said Winston Churchill on the day when Hitler was discussing with Mussolini the armistice terms to be imposed on France, 'is over. I expect that the Battle of Britain is about to begin.' And he went on to exhort his fellow-countrymen so to bear themselves that, if the British Empire lasted for a thousand years, men would still say: 'This was their finest hour.'

By the end of August, heavy fighting between Britain's air defences and the Luftwaffe—or what seemed like heavy fighting—had been going on for six weeks. Apparently the battle predicted by Churchill had begun and was in progress. But it did not seem much like a battle to those who were not fighting. This was not so much because it was being fought, so to speak, on London's doorstep, or because it had already gone on for a long time without bringing a decision, as for other reasons. Many important actions had been fought near large cities, and the public was used to hearing the long-drawn infantry and artillery duels of the First World War described as battles. The so-called battles of the Somme and Passchendaele had led to inconsiderable gains and appalling casualties; but at least it had been possible to read of villages or natural features lost or taken, and even to make some play with pins and flags. Where the struggle now in progress differed from past encounters was that, in spite of a well-founded impression that momentous decisions were impending, little that was tangible ever seemed to happen. Indeed, it was difficult to guess even what might be going to happen. Obviously great issues were at stake: the statesmen said so. But what exactly were they, and how near were they to decision?

For the man in the street to follow the progress of the Battle of Britain while it was being fought was, in fact, impossible. News bulletins made the most of the numbers of German aircraft supposedly destroyed in each day's fighting; but most people wisely refused to read more into these figures than a welcome indication that the air defences were giving better than they got. A bare announcement that the enemy had lost a hundred aircraft meant little—even if it was accurate—unless one knew what his resources were, what reserves he had and how fast he could make good his losses from new production. Whether the Germans were drawing nearer the right conditions for a landing in Britain—if that was their object—there was no means of telling, except that they did not come. British journalists and compilers of broadcast bulletins prided themselves on not telling lies; but the whole truth could not be told in wartime, and the effect of censorship was often to play down damage to military objectives with results seen in retrospect to be almost ludicrously misleading. Members of the public informed that a couple of houses had been demolished at a seaside resort, and that 'only a few civilians' had been killed, could not be expected to guess—and were not expected to guess—that the bomb which did the damage was one of many aimed at a neighbouring aerodrome, and that most of the others had hit the target, destroying scores of aircraft and reducing hangars to a Chinese puzzle of twisted girders.

As for personal observation, a fair number of citizens saw damage done by bombing near their homes or at the places where they worked, and were sometimes angered by discrepancies between the evidence of their own eyes and accounts in the newspapers. Otherwise little could be seen or heard of actions fought three or four miles above the southern counties. Occasionally watchers on the ground had a grandstand view of the fighting, especially in the early stages when many attacks were made on Channel convoys near the coast; later, when the Germans took to sending their fighters over at high altitudes, the sight of vapour-trails became familiar. More often, nothing was visible except, at most, a few specks in the sky, too high up even for the sound of engines to be heard except when a queer trick of acoustics caused the roar of an aircraft diving in order to shake off a pursuer, or because it was out of control, to shatter the silence as suddenly as if the noise had been produced by some cosmic conjurer like a rabbit from a hat. Apart from these signs, and the daily test-match scores in the newspapers and on the wireless, hardly anything was seen or heard of the fighting except an occasional burst of machine-gun fire which seemed to come from nowhere,

THE BATTLE OF BRITAIN

occasionally the spine-chilling whistle of falling bombs culminating in an awe-inspiring series of explosions, and, for a few favoured citizens, the rare sight of a shot-down pilot still in flying-kit re-joining his unit by public transport. Men and women who lived where German aircraft were reported to be falling thick and fast remarked sometimes in the privacy of their homes that they scarcely ever saw one.

Even the best informed observers had difficulty in knowing what was happening. When neutral journalists questioned the accuracy of the combat figures published by the Air Ministry—which did, in fact, give an unwittingly false picture of German losses—Dowding replied that the claims made by his pilots might, or might not, be correct, but at any rate were not wilfully misleading. Whether the claims made by the other side were accurate, he added for the benefit of the journalists and the American Ambassador, would soon be known because, if they were, the Germans would be in London in a week. And that was about as far as anyone could go until, in early September, air reconnaissance threw new light on the state of Hitler's preparations for invasion.

As for the men who did the fighting, by the end of August most pilots in the active sectors in south-eastern England had ceased to worry about the overall strategic picture, if indeed they ever did. They knew that for them, at any rate, the fighting had reached a crisis: beyond that they could not look. This was not because they were the tough, uncaring figments of a strip-cartoonist's imagination which they were sometimes supposed to be, but because they had become keyed up to such a pitch of concentration on the business in hand that almost everything outside the daily struggle for survival had become unimportant. It was not so much that other concerns had ceased to interest them as that they had come to regard almost everything but their unceasing struggle with the Luftwaffe as taking place at a lower pitch of consciousness, to which they would find it hard to attune themselves while the battle lasted. 'I can't help feeling', said one of them only half jokingly when he and the rest of his squadron were taking the occasional day off enjoined by Dowding, 'that this is a case of Nero fiddling while Rome is burning.'

In some ways the inability of the man in the street to gauge the state

35 *German invasion-barges at Dunkirk, Summer, 1940*

36   *3.7-inch mobile A.A. gun in action*

37   *A south-coast beach, Summer, 1940*

BRITISH ANTI-AIRCRAFT AND BEACH DEFENCES

of the battle was no bad thing, for he would not have found the outlook at the end of August reassuring. Dowding's squadrons were still fighting magnificently, and were to go on fighting magnificently, but effectively their strength was dwindling. Faced with the more closely-knit formations the Luftwaffe was now using, they were losing more aircraft and pilots than they could afford, and were shooting down too few bombers to make it probable that Göring would call off his offensive while he saw a hope of victory. The veterans who had borne the brunt of the fighting since Dunkirk were tiring; the inexperienced newcomers who replaced those killed, wounded or posted away were a source of weakness at a time when no squadron in an active sector could afford to carry passengers. In spite of the widely-held theory that bombing aerodromes was a waste of time, the attacks on Park's sector stations were a powerful threat to their efficiency. Göring's bad start had cost him his chance of doing everything he had planned to do in the few weeks he allowed himself, but he still had time to achieve his first aim by smashing the fighter defences in the south of England before the question of invasion or no invasion had to be decided.

In some ways Dowding's anxieties during the next week or so were even more crushing than Park's, not merely because his responsibilities were wider and because he was preoccupied with the problem of the night bomber, but because he was uncomfortably aware that there was hardly anything he could do to ease Park's lot. The wholesale milking of squadrons in quiet sectors of their best pilots for the benefit of the active sectors, for which Park pressed, he regarded as a desperate expedient to be adopted only in a supreme emergency; for squadrons left without at least a nucleus of first-rate officers would cease, in effect, to be first-line squadrons, and might be a fatal source of weakness if the war took a new turn before they could be nursed back to their old status. Nor could he, without sacrificing the advantages of the control system, use entire squadrons from quiet sectors to increase Park's strength beyond the number of squadrons his sectors could handle—and that number was likely to grow smaller rather than larger as more and more stations were bombed and perhaps forced to rely on standby operations rooms.

On the other hand there was comfort for Dowding, though not

much for Park, in the knowledge that there was still a valuable reserve of intact squadrons outside No. 11 Group, and that enough of them could be concentrated within reach of London to make a useful contribution to its defence if and when the focus of the enemy's daylight offensive shifted inland. In the meantime Park could, and did, call on squadrons in Brand's and Leigh-Mallory's flanking sectors for tactical reinforcement when his group was threatened. The value of this help was, however, limited by the difficulty of controlling squadrons far from their parent sectors, and by a recurrent clash between Leigh-Mallory's determination that his squadrons should play a leading role in the battle and Park's insistence that they should think first of guarding his stations north of the Thames Estuary. Whereas Park found Brand's squadrons extremely useful, he complained, not without some reason, that Leigh-Mallory's hardly ever went where he wanted them to go and were always turning up in places where he and his controllers had no means of keeping track of them.

But the enemy also had his troubles. Göring's squadrons, some of them making several sorties a day over England, were tiring, too. They were driven harder than Dowding's because there was no one on the German side who both shared his conviction that fatigue meant heavy losses and had the power and the will to act on it. A German commander who suggested resting first-line crews while the battle was at its height would have found himself in the same trouble as Dowding had experienced twenty-four years earlier on the Somme. A German staff officer who did, in fact, make some such suggestion to his chief was left in no doubt that he would be unwise to press the matter. On both sides, over-estimation of the enemy's losses hid the true state of affairs; but the Germans were far worse deceived than their opponents, not so much because the British tried harder to check their pilots' claims (although they did) as because the German Air Staff, unlike the British, made the mistake of basing their estimates of the enemy's effective strength on this notoriously untrustworthy evidence. In consequence they consistently underestimated British capabilities; and German fighter pilots and bomber crews felt anything but reassured when they found that the enemy could put almost as many fighters over Kent and Sussex in one operation as he was supposed to be able to muster in the whole of the United Kingdom.

On August 30, after a day of fighter sweeps on the 29th, Kessel-ring's bombers returned in force to attack Biggin Hill, the Vauxhall factory at Luton, in Bedfordshire, and Coastal Command's much-bombed aerodrome at Detling. For the first time, Fighter Command flew more than a thousand sorties—a great shock for German aircrew who had just been told that the battle was as good as won and that the British had scarcely any fighters left. On the other hand, Park's squadrons did not succeed in beating off the attacks, as was claimed by the newspapers, and damage to all three objectives was severe. A formation which bombed Biggin Hill in the morning was inter-cepted only on the homeward route; in the afternoon the bombers bound for Luton were met near Sheppey, and some were forced to jettison their bombs, but the rest were not prevented from going on to the target and making a fairly accurate attack which killed about fifty civilians at Luton airport and in the town. At Detling, too, an attack which put the aerodrome out of use for fifteen hours followed an accurate but largely ineffective interception.

Worse still, under cover of the attack on Luton a squadron of bombers reached Biggin Hill unexpectedly by suddenly turning south from the main stream, and followed up the morning's raid with devastating accuracy, wrecking workshops, stores and hangars, severing power, gas and water mains, and killing or wounding sixty-five of the station staff. About the only satisfactory feature of a black day for Fighter Command was the destruction of thirty-six German aircraft. They included a bomber shot down by a Polish pilot, Pilot-Officer L. Pasckiewicz, on a training flight, and one inadvertently rammed by a South African, Flight-Lieutenant E. J. Morris, who baled out, emerged unscathed from his David-and-Goliath contest, and found himself the hero of many legends, the most widely believed of which was that he had intentionally collided with his victim when his guns jammed.

In the light of these experiences Park took special care on August 31 to guard his sector stations, but again without much success because the German fighter escorts were too strong for his pilots to get through to the bombers. The Luftwaffe's targets for the day were Park's aerodromes at Debden, Hornchurch, Biggin Hill and Croydon; Leigh-Mallory's sector station at Duxford; and Coastal Command's aerodrome at Eastchurch.

Duxford was saved, according to one account, by the Hurricanes of No. 111 Squadron which intercepted the approaching bombers over Essex; according to another, by nine aircraft of No. 19 Squadron, led by Flight-Lieutenant W. G. Clouston, which met them near the target and were able to fire a few rounds before the experimental cannon in the wings of their Spitfires jammed. The bombs meant for Duxford were scattered over Essex, Suffolk and Cambridgeshire.

Park's stations were not so lucky. At Hornchurch three pilots of No. 54 Squadron, Flying-Officer A. C. Deere, Pilot-Officer Edsell and Sergeant Davies, were just taking off, and had reached a height of about twenty feet, when a stick of bombs fell immediately in front of them. Deere's Spitfire was thrown on to its back, and raced upside down across the aerodrome at a hundred miles an hour for some distance before coming to rest in a position which gave the pilot no chance of getting out without help. Edsell crashed the right way up with his legs so badly hurt that he could not stand, but he managed to crawl across and rescue Deere, who had only a flesh-wound. Meanwhile Davies's aircraft had been blown clean out of the aerodrome, and no more was seen of him until he turned up, unhurt, two hours later, after walking half-way round the station to find a way in.

At Biggin Hill everyone from the Station Commander to a boy bugler borrowed from a local volunteer organisation to help the signals staff was keyed up to expect another visit after the previous day's attacks; but the bombers bound for the station nevertheless achieved some measure of tactical surprise by flying towards Kenley and then suddenly turning north-east a few miles from the target. The operations room was not protected by a comforting layer of earth and concrete like those at Stanmore and Uxbridge; but W.A.A.F. plotters and telephone-operators, apparently unmoved, went on calmly receiving and marking plots right up to the moment when the bombers were overhead. One of the first bombs cut all the telephone-lines connecting the operations rooms with the rest of the station, and the watch, unable to do anything more to help the fighters, were ordered to take what cover they could find. Sergeant Helen Turner and Corporal Elspeth Henderson, refusing to leave their posts, continued to man the still-uncut line to Uxbridge. A few seconds after Sergeant Turner had been dragged, still pro-testing, from the switchboard, a bomb came through the roof, putting out the lights, filling the room with acrid dust and smoke, and showering the place where she had been sitting with slivers of jagged metal. Group-Captain Grice, entering at that moment to see how the watch was getting on, was cut about the face and hands by splinters from a glass plotting-screen, had his pipe knocked out of his mouth but deftly retrieved it in the dark, and picked up the unhurt but shaken Corporal Henderson, who brushed aside his compliment on her composure with the comment that she had joined the service to see a bit of life. The only casualty, apart from minor injuries, was the boy bugler, who died three days later from the effects of blast.

Even so, the attack was an almost crippling blow for Park. To a lesser extent, so too were the attacks on Hornchurch and Debden. By nightfall Fighter Command had lost thirty-nine aircraft in combat since morning to the Luftwaffe's forty-one, besides at least ten Spitfires destroyed by bombing or burnt out on the ground. At Debden damage to buildings was particularly heavy. At Biggin Hill, where the previous day's dead were still unburied and where life was becoming a tough and uncomfortable business for the survivors, the operations block was a blackened shell and the general state of things was such that Park had no choice but to withdraw two squadrons, leaving one to be controlled in makeshift fashion from a shop in the village until a new operations block could be got going in a requisitioned villa. On top of this, at least one of his squadrons, No. 56, had been so badly knocked about in the air fighting that it had to be not merely moved to a quiet sector but taken out of the line until it could be re-equipped and brought up to strength again.

In consequence, the beginning of September found Göring within measurable distance of his goal. With Manston already out of use except for emergency landings, and West Malling, Lympne and Hawkinge more or less untenable, he had had only to repeat at Tangmere and Kenley what he had done at Biggin Hill, adding Westhampnett, Croydon and Gravesend as a precaution against their adoption as alternative sector stations, to make it almost impossible for Park to carry on the defence of London from stations south of London. Even then it did not necessarily follow that Göring would win, for a stout defence could still be made from stations north of the Thames and further west, and sooner or later other aerodromes south of the river might be pressed into service. But air superiority over Kent and Sussex for at least a week or two would be well within Göring's grasp, and the rest might follow. To drive his opponent out of these five stations, three of them already badly damaged, and keep him out of them and Biggin Hill for a limited period, as he was already keeping him out of Manston, was an undertaking which ought not to have been beyond his powers if he grasped the supreme importance of concentrating on it to the exclusion of all other aims.

But this was just what Göring did not grasp. At a moment of supreme crisis for both sides he was undone, as he had been undone at the beginning of the battle, by his inability to turn his back on inessentials. Had he made up his mind, on the morning of Sunday, September 1, to devote his entire effort for the next week to the subjection of the Kenley, Biggin Hill and Tangmere sectors, he could not have failed to set Park and Dowding a problem which would have taxed them to the utmost.

As it was, Group-Captain Grice was burying his dead that Sunday morning when the one squadron left to him took off to counter the fifth attack on Biggin Hill since Friday; and the eighth, and last, raid of a series which drove him to the heroic expedient of blowing up a damaged but outwardly intact hangar lest it attract more bombs was not made until another four days of constant anxiety had passed. But meanwhile other, equally important stations went unscathed while the Germans wasted bombs on aircraft factories whose destruction could not conceivably affect the Royal Air Force for many weeks. On the 4th the Luftwaffe attacked the Vickers-Armstrong factory near Weybridge, which made bombers; on the 6th the Hawker factory on the other side of Brooklands aerodrome. The argument that the deep penetration entailed by such raids gave more scope for air combat looked good on paper; but it did not appeal to Kesselring's fighter pilots, who hated having to fight at extreme range, with the knowledge that they would probably come down in the Channel if they failed to break off promptly.

Even so, eight days of crisis for Fighter Command did bring fairly good results from the point of view of the German fighter force. In active operations between August 30 and September 6 the command lost a hundred and eighty-five aircraft to the Luftwaffe's two hundred and twenty-five. If forty to fifty German aircraft which crash-landed on the way home can be deducted—which is doubtful, for probably most of them would have landed safely at base if they had not been in contact with the enemy—then the Luftwaffe's claim that the air fighting went in their favour was justified for the first time since the beginning of the battle.

To defend not only their own bases and Coastal Command's aerodromes at Eastchurch and Detling, but also the half-dozen aircraft factories and miscellaneous objectives included in the German target-list, Park's squadrons fought with almost desperate energy and courage during that anxious week. Most pilots, apart from those belonging to a few squadrons brought in from quiet sectors, were feeling the strain of fighting almost daily, and some-times several times a day, since midsummer. Michael Constable Maxwell, a pilot of No. 56 Squadron at North Weald, and son of a father well known to two generations of his fellow-airmen, went through an experience which was symptomatic though exceptional. On August 30 he was shot down for the third time since Dunkirk. At one thousand feet over Herne Bay his engine stopped. Unwilling to jump out with the knowledge that, if he did, his aircraft would probably crash into houses, he stayed in the cockpit, expecting the aircraft to burst into flames at any moment, made a landing of sorts in a field bounded by a road lined with telegraph poles, and escaped unhurt from the wreckage. Hatless and dirty, he made the tedious journey back to his base on the other side of the Thames Estuary by train, arriving six hours after take-off to learn that his brother Andrew had also been shot down. The taxi-driver who took him across London refused a tip, saying that he would be ashamed to accept one from a man who had just risked his life for him. And that, perhaps, was how most people would have felt.

Yet, in spite of the strain on Park's pilots, and in spite of his gnawing dread of a series of further blows which might put his sector stations out of commission for the next stage of the battle, there were features of the German effort which deserve a little study.

In the first four days of heavy fighting in mid-August, the Luft-waffe flew a daily average of roughly fifteen hundred sorties. On the four days which followed Göring's decision to limit daylight bomber operations in good weather to those for which strong escort could be provided, the average fell to about nine hundred, a quiet day on August 27 excluded. From August 30, with less than a fortnight to go to the date, already once postponed, when the Führer was due to decide whether the offensive had fulfilled its purpose, and with victory in sight if General von Döring was to be believed, the Luftwaffe had every reason not to pull its punches. By driving units to the limit in spite of one or two protests from subordinates, commanders did, in fact, achieve more than thirteen hundred sorties on August 30 and more than fourteen hundred on the 31st. But the fall thereafter was striking and significant. Irrespective of what Fighter Command had suffered, the effect on the Luftwaffe of losing more than eight hundred aircraft in two months was not far short of shattering. On September 1 the Germans flew only six hundred and forty sorties; on none of the next five days did the figure reach a thousand. By September 6 Dowding's squadrons were flying not only many more sorties than the German fighter force, but more than the German bomber and fighter forces put together. The reason was not obvious at the time, but it is clear enough today. At the moment when a supreme effort was essential if Hitler was not to come to the conclusion that Göring's 'undreamt-of might' had failed him, Kesselring was down to about four hundred and fifty serviceable long-range bombers and five hundred and thirty short-range fighters, with another sixty to seventy fighters more or less at his disposal on Sperrle's aerodromes.

10

On The Brink

HAD GÖRING BEEN Commander-in-Chief of the Luftwaffe in fact as well as theory, and had he been an able man, he would probably have spent the last two days of August and the first few of September making sure that his subordinate commanders understood the paramount importance of knocking out Park's sector stations south of London. He would have taken care that, for at least a week, not a bomb was aimed in daylight at any target except the fighter stations in those sectors.

As it was, he devoted himself to preparations for the next stage of the offensive.

The new programme, outlined in a preliminary instruction on August 31 and further defined in a formal directive on September 2, reflected a wish expressed privately by Hitler on August 30 to carry out concentrated attacks on London as reprisals for Bomber Command's raid on Berlin on the night of August 25. It also reflected both Göring's itch to reduce the British Government and people to acquiescence by the time the German Navy's invasion preparations were complete, and the opinion of his advisers that the best way of finishing off Fighter Command was to go for so supremely important and vulnerable an objective that Dowding would be forced to throw in his reserve of supposedly uncommitted squadrons. 'Dowding is cautious', the Germans argued in effect, 'and is keeping something back. If we attack London, the Government will insist on his bringing south his squadrons in the north and Midlands, and we shall destroy them as we are now destroying those in Kent and Sussex.' But they failed to remind themselves that the squadrons in Kent and Sussex were still, in fact, a long way from destruction.

In a speech at the Sportspalast in Berlin on September 4, two days after Göring had issued his directive, Hitler publicly threatened the

British with 'extermination of their cities'. Next day a directive from Supreme Headquarters called for 'harassing attacks by day and night on the inhabitants and air defences of large British cities', and added that London was to be among them.

For the purposes of the round-the-clock offensive, London was divided into two target-areas, both to be attacked at night by Luftflotte 3 and in daylight by Luftflotte 2. Target-area A was the East End, where the chief objectives were in and round the docks. Target-area B, where the objectives were mostly public utility undertakings, coincided more or less with the rest of London. General Hans Jeschonnek, Chief of Staff of the Luftwaffe, was eager that residential districts should be included in order to spread panic, and was backed, rather surprisingly, by Raeder; but Hitler forbade this, insisting that attacks on military objectives were always the most effective, and that bombing 'with the object of causing a mass panic' was a last resort. Like their counterparts in London, German ministers and officials were blissfully unaware that bomber crews on both sides had about as much chance of hitting precise objectives in a well-defended built-up area at night as a blind dart-player has of throwing a double twenty. Except in daylight, it made no practical difference whether residential districts were included in the target-list or not, because they were sure to be hit in any case.

The attack on London was timed to begin on September 7. On the night of the 4th German aircraft dropped flares over London, presumably for purposes of reconnaissance and perhaps also to rub in the lesson of Hitler's speech. On the next two nights a few bombs were dropped in dockland areas. Since no one in England knew that the bombing of London on the night of August 24 was unintentional, no special significance was attached to these events, and the speech was regarded as just another example of the Führer's habit of uttering threats which he might, or might not, mean to carry out.

On September 7 Sperrle had just over three hundred serviceable long-range bombers ready for his night offensive. To augment the four hundred and fifty serviceable long-range bombers at Kessel-ring's disposal for attacks in daylight, the incomplete Kampfgeschwader 26 and 30 were brought south from Denmark and Norway and put under his command; but their strength and serviceability were very low, and they added fewer than forty usable aircraft to the total. At the same time most of the available dive-bombers were concentrated under Kesselring near the Straits of Dover, where they would be ready to support a landing if the invasion fleet did sail. Göring's directive expressly ordered Kesselring to supplement the six hundred serviceable short-range fighters in his command or at his disposal by using long-range fighters, of which he had about a hundred fit for use. Altogether, about thirteen hundred serviceable bombers, dive-bombers and fighters of all types were available for daylight operations, as compared with well over two thousand on Eagle Day. But this total included about two hundred and twenty Junkers 87s and Messerschmitt 110s which were so vulnerable unless accompanied by large numbers of short-range fighters as to be more of a liability than an asset.

In practice, Kesselring was not likely to send more than about two-thirds of his bombers across the Channel at one time, because his six hundred short-range fighters were too few to support a substantially larger number. To match these, Park had twenty-one squadrons of Hurricanes and Spitfires, and could call on his neighbours to reinforce him with perhaps nine more at the most—a grand total of about three hundred to three hundred and fifty aircraft if he threw in everything he had. If Kesselring came in strength, Park would certainly be outnumbered. On the other hand, the extreme range at which the German fighters would be working was a handicap which no experienced commander could contemplate without dismay. On the form shown by both sides since Dunkirk, a shrewd punter with all the facts before him would probably have decided to back Park.

Meanwhile, Park had no means of knowing that his opponents were about to do him the favour of switching their attack to London. His chief concern on the eve of the new phase was still for his sector stations. In the light of his experiences in recent weeks, detachments of Royal Engineers now stood by at more than twenty aerodromes in the south of England to fill in craters and clear rubble; the Air Ministry had set up special Works Repair Depots in many places; and arrangements had been made for damage to landlines to be made good at short notice by Post Office engineers and army signallers. To protect his stations as far as possible from further bombing, he decided that, when those south of the Thames were threatened, he would send most of his available squadrons forward to meet the enemy near the coast, in pairs if there was time to form them, keeping back a few as a second line of defence for Kenley, Biggin Hill and Croydon.

After the bombing of the Vickers-Armstrong factory on September 4, Dowding warned Park that he must pay special attention to the defence of aircraft factories west of London. To meet this new commitment, Park decided to make use of reinforcing squadrons from No. 10 Group, which would come east from the Middle Wallop sector to patrol a line from Windsor to Brooklands. To protect his stations north of the Thames he would rely largely on Leigh-Mallory, who was more than willing to contribute up to five squadrons drawn from his Duxford and Wittering sectors. Park would have felt happier about the help to be expected from No. 12 Group if Leigh-Mallory, largely at the prompting of the indomitable legless pilot Squadron-Leader Douglas Bader, had not enthusiastically taken up the idea that the most effective way of using his reinforcing squadrons was to send them south in wings of two, three, four or five squadrons. In principle, Park had nothing against such formations: he was planning to use his own squadrons in pairs, and had used wings of up to four squadrons at Dunkirk. But he feared that, if Leigh-Mallory spent ten or fifteen minutes assembling a large wing over Duxford, his pilots would arrive too late, as had happened at Debden on August 26 when only a single squadron had been sent. He therefore gave orders that some of the squadrons in the North Weald, Debden and Hornchurch sectors should be held back to guard their bases until the reinforcing squadrons turned up to relieve them.

The Germans launched the new phase of their offensive late in the afternoon on Saturday, September 7. Watched by Göring himself from a point of vantage within sight of the English coast, more than three hundred bombers and about six hundred short-range and long-range fighters streamed across the Channel to deliver the first big daylight attack on London. Except that the dive-bombers were held back for lack of range and because they were so vulnerable, the effort was about the largest of which Kesselring was capable.

The bombers and fighters took so long to assemble that ample warning was received at Uxbridge that German aircraft were massing over France. Park was away from his headquarters, attending a conference at Stanmore. But the officers who took turns as group

38   *Fires at Purfleet after the first September raid on London*

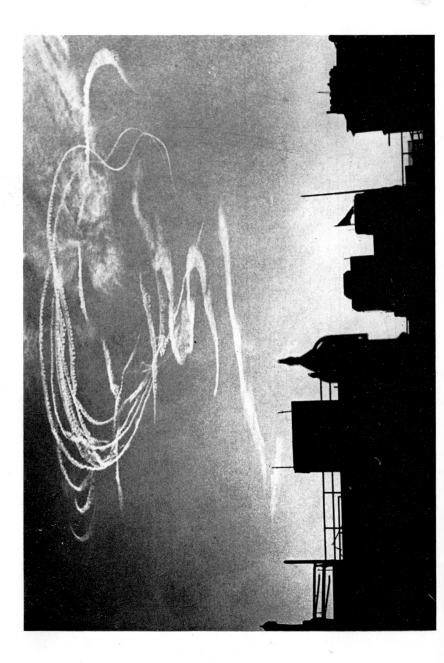

controller in his operations room were experts at the interception game, and were well briefed. There was no special reason to suppose that things would go wrong in the group commander's absence.

Nor was a daylight attack on London so unlikely as to be an unexpected hazard. Apart from the bombing of dockland areas on each of the last two nights, the docks at Tilbury, only twenty miles from Tower Bridge, had been bombed in daylight on September 1, and oil refineries at Thames Haven, a few miles further down the river, on the 5th and 6th. On the other side of London the aircraft factories at Brooklands, attacked on the 4th and 6th, were barely eighteen miles from Hyde Park Corner.

Nevertheless, things did go wrong, although that was not necessarily the group controller's fault. Presumably reckoning that the enemy's line of approach was too far east to suggest a heavy attack on sector stations south of London, and that therefore the plan of sending pairs of squadrons forward did not apply, he put only single squadrons or smaller formations over various points in Surrey, Kent and Sussex, and concentrated largely on protecting likely objectives further north. Among these were Thames Haven, where fires started by the recent attacks were still burning, and sector stations north of the Thames Estuary. All this was reasonable enough in view of the obvious danger that Hornchurch and North Weald might suffer the same fate as Biggin Hill, or that Luton might be attacked again. A controller with no group commander to consult could hardly be blamed if he erred on the side of caution. But the result was that well over half the fighters airborne when the enemy arrived—among them a two-squadron wing sent from Northolt to patrol north-east of London—were too far north to stand a chance of catching him before his leading bombers reached their targets. As things turned out, it would have paid the controller better to make a bolder use of squadrons from the northern sectors, and rely more on three squadrons coming south from No. 12 Group to intervene if the enemy pushed on north of London. Visibility was good, and Leigh-Mallory's squadrons, even if they could not always be trusted to intercept small formations bound for aerodromes, were hardly likely to miss a big one on its way to a target such as Luton. On the other hand, this may have been just what the controller feared might happen.

Among the first bombers to reach London, if not the first of all, were the Dornier 17s of Kampfgeschwader 2, led by Fink in person and bound for Poplar and Canning Town with orders to bomb the Royal Victoria Dock and the East or West India Docks, or both. By all accounts a God-fearing man, not given to joking about serious matters, Fink is said to have had a habit of telling crews to make their wills. The advice must have seemed particularly apt when, twenty miles short of the target according to Fink's recollection, his close escort of Messerschmitt 109s turned back for fear of running out of fuel. But only a handful of British squadrons were anywhere near his route, and his formation reached the neighbourhood of its objectives without much opposition. Some of those which followed had a rougher passage, but most combats took place after the bombers had dropped their loads, or when they were so near their objectives that even jettisoned bombs did heavy damage.

By the time the raid was over, nearly an hour and a half after it began, more than three hundred tons of high-explosive had fallen on and round London in broad daylight. Seventeen of Park's squadrons, besides three of Leigh-Mallory's and one of Brand's, had gone into action and had shot down most of the forty-one German bombers lost. But failure to head the bombers off, and the loss of forty-four British fighters destroyed or badly damaged and seventeen pilots killed or seriously wounded, amounted to a serious set-back for Park and Dowding. The bombing was nothing like as accurate as the Germans believed, for many crews aimed short; but the districts on both banks of the Thames from Rotherhithe to Barking were so vulnerable that the effects were almost worse than if they had hit their targets. Apart from damage to the docks, an area about a mile and half long and half a mile wide on the north bank of the river at Bugsby's Reach was devastated, and the inhabitants of Silvertown were cut off by fire and had to be rescued in barges, tugs and boats. Further east, more fires were started at Thames Haven; elsewhere there was damage as far west as Kensington, and as far north and south as Tottenham and Croydon.

The first big daylight raid on London since 1917 caused intense excitement. The usual crop of rumours sprang up in newspaper offices, clubs, canteens and private dwellings. Their aftermath was the belief, still widely held long after the war was over, that the Government were stampeded into a groundless fear that German troops were about to land in Britain, and were led to order panic measures.

In point of fact, the machinery of government functioned precisely as usual, except that one or two officials and service chiefs were held up on their way to or from conferences by traffic delays arising from the raid, or because their drivers had taken shelter and they could not find their cars. No important decision was taken by, or on behalf of, the Government which would not have been taken irrespective of the raid.

As it happened, September 7 would have been a red-letter day in British governmental and official circles even if the Luftwaffe had not chosen it for their first daylight raid on London.

For weeks past an inter-service working committee, the Combined Intelligence Committee, had been reporting daily to the Joint Intelligence Sub-Committee of the Chiefs of Staff Committee on the state of German preparations for invasion. Their information was derived mainly, but not wholly, from photographic reconnaissance of the North Sea ports and Channel ports from the Texel to Cherbourg.

Up to the end of August the Combined Intelligence Committee had little to report, because air photographs gave no indication that German preparations were well advanced. But photographs taken in the next few days told a different story. On September 4, for example, they showed that something like a hundred barges, presumably intended to carry German troops to England, had reached Flushing alone since the beginning of the month; on the 7th, that the number at Ostend had increased by more than two hundred and fifty since the last day of August, and that substantial numbers had also arrived at Dunkirk, Calais and elsewhere. Furthermore, the transfer of Stumpff's long-range bombers to Kesselring's command had been spotted, and Kesselring was known to be concentrating his dive-bombers near the Straits. Another significant item of intelligence was that four Germans caught landing from a rowing-boat had confessed that they were spies, and that their mission was to report British troop movements which would be of obvious interest to a landing-force.

According to British experts, moon and tide would specially favour a landing in Britain between September 8 and 10. The Combined Intelligence Committee therefore reported on the

7th—many hours before the daylight raid on London—that invasion might be imminent. The Joint Intelligence Committee passed the report on to the Chiefs of Staff for consideration at a meeting to be held that afternoon.

About the time when Kesselring's first bombs were falling at Woolwich and the Isle of Dogs, the Chiefs of Staff sat down in Whitehall to consider, among other matters, the report from the Combined Intelligence Committee. General Sir Alan Brooke, commanding Home Forces, would normally have been called in for consultation, but was out of London. His place was taken by his Chief of Staff, Lieutenant-General Bernard Paget.

The Chiefs of Staff did not know that the time had come when German troops would, in fact, have been landing between Ramsgate and Lyme Bay if Brauchitsch had been able to carry out his original programme and if Hitler had given the preliminary order for invasion on the date first planned. Nor did they know that the programme had been held up and that Hitler did not now contemplate a landing before the 21st. On the evidence before them, they had no choice but to conclude that a landing within the next day or two was extremely probable, and that failure to guard against the danger would be madness.

On the British side, the situation when the Chiefs of Staff began their meeting at 5.20 p.m. was that the Royal Navy was ready to resist invasion to its utmost capacity, except that the Home Fleet was still at Scapa Flow. In deference to the views of the Commander-in-Chief, Sir Charles Forbes, the Admiralty had agreed that it should remain there unless a move to Rosyth became imperative, and that Forbes should send his heavy ships southward to assist in breaking up a landing on the east coast only if German heavy ships were definitely known to be at sea. The Royal Air Force, too, was as ready as it could be made except on receipt of definite news that the German invasion fleet had sailed. The problem which troubled the Chiefs of Staff was that General Brooke's troops, on the other hand, were not at 'instant readiness' but at eight hours' notice, except that they stood-to daily at dawn and dusk, and that no provision had been made to bring them to a higher degree of readiness, short of issuing the signal 'Cromwell', which meant 'invasion imminent'.

Was invasion imminent? In a sense it was, or at least appeared to be in the light of the report from the Combined Intelligence

Committee. In consultation with General Paget the Chiefs of Staff agreed, therefore, if not specifically that the 'Cromwell' signal should be sent, at any rate that troops in Eastern and Southern Commands should be called to the highest attainable degree of readiness by the only means available.

This decision taken, Paget left the meeting with the intention of giving effect to it, and was promptly swallowed up in the confusion caused by the raid then at its height. Unlike his chief, he kept no diary, and his movements are obscure; but it seems clear from the evidence of his deputy, Brigadier John Swayne (afterwards Lieutenant-General Sir John Swayne) that he did not get back to G.H.Q. at Hammersmith until some hours later, or at any rate that Swayne did not see him.

Meanwhile Swayne, too, had digested the report from the Combined Intelligence Committee, and may, or may not, have discussed it with Paget before Paget left for the meeting of the Chiefs of Staff. He, in his turn, saw no way of meeting the situation except by sending the 'Cromwell' signal. According to his unshakeable recollection, his decision to send it was taken on his own responsibility and without express authority from Brooke or Paget. At any rate it is a fact that, at 8.7 p.m., G.H.Q. sent the signal to Eastern and Southern Commands, the two corps in G.H.Q. Reserve, and formations in the London area, repeating it to other commands for information only.

It was not Swayne's fault, nor was it Brooke's or Paget's, that some of the consequences were unforeseen. On receiving the signal some commanders decided on their own responsibility to call out the Home Guard. Some Home Guard commanders took it upon themselves, with even less authority, to summon their men by causing church bells to be rung. As this was the agreed signal that paratroopers had been seen descending, the effect was to create an atmosphere in which all kinds of rumours flourished. Well-intentioned persons, and perhaps some not so well intentioned, spread stories to the effect that the Germans were already landing or had landed, that they were crossing the North Sea or the Channel in fast motor-boats, and so on. Sober citizens, hastening to joint their Home Guard detachments, took leave of their wives and children in affecting circumstances, many not expecting to see their families again until the war was over, if at all.

All this led to a good deal of resentment when the excitements of the 7th were followed by anti-climax. Members of the Home Guard who found themselves back at home within twelve hours of saying farewell for the duration of the war were angry with the authorities whom they blamed for making them look foolish. The high-ups in Whitehall, they said, ought not to have sanctioned the sending of the 'Cromwell' signal when there was no evidence that the invasion fleet had sailed or even that the Germans had embarked. Some accused the Government, then or later, of panicking. They were thrown off balance, said their critics, by the daylight raid on London.

These complaints were misconceived and misdirected. The calling of troops to instant readiness was fully justified on the evidence available at the time; and the 'Cromwell' signal was the only way of doing it. The high-ups in Whitehall were not responsible for the calling out of the Home Guard, which they did not authorise. Nor were they answerable for the ringing of church bells, expressly forbidden except as a warning that paratroops had been seen. The Government did not panic. They were not stampeded by the air raid. The 'Cromwell' signal would still have been sent even if there had been no raid. If the raid affected its despatch at all, it did so only to the extent of delaying it for an hour or two and causing it to be sent by Swayne instead of Paget.

As the last of Kesselring's bombers turned for home that Saturday evening, the first of Sperrle's were warming up for the night attack that followed. At half-past eight the leaders reached the target, guided by the immense fires raging in the East End and further down the river at Thames Haven. By half-past four on Sunday morning, when the last bomber was on its way home or had landed, another three hundred tons of high-explosive and thousands of small incendiary bombs had fallen within ten miles of Charing Cross, three main-line termini were out of action, practically all rail traffic in and out of London to the south had ceased to run, and many Londoners had lost their lives in addition to those killed earlier.

The defences were powerless to stop Sperrle's two hundred and fifty bombers. Of the two specialist night-fighter squadrons in No. 11 Group, one could not get off the ground because its base at Hornchurch was blanketed in smoke; the other, at Martlesham, sent two Blenheims to patrol north-east of London for three hours before midnight, and a third to take their place in the early morning, but all three crews drew blank. The experimental Fighter Interception Unit south of London put up a Blenheim and a Beaufighter, both with airborne radar, but they were equally unsuccessful. General Pile's guns, forbidden to fire at targets not seen or specifically located, were hopelessly handicapped by out-of-date equipment. Parts of the system went out of action for long periods because communications failed, and many citizens were roused to indignation by the lack of gunfire. Dowding was right when he pointed out that, strategically, the night offensive was relatively unimportant because, unlike the daylight offensive, it could not give the Germans a decision. But such things, as he would have been the first to recognize, could not be said to a man who had seen his children buried in a heap of rubble, or to a poor widow bombed out of her home with the loss of every stick of furniture she had and every penny of her savings.

Next day Dowding made a significant decision. Faced with the results of the daylight fighting on the 7th, he agreed at last that squadrons in the active sectors in No. 11 Group and on its flanks must have the pick of the command's best pilots, irrespective of the effect on other squadrons. In a sense the decision did no more than sanction an existing tendency to give preference to those squadrons which had come to be recognised as the best-led and most experienced. The step was nevertheless a difficult one for Dowding to take in view of his reluctance to draw such hard-and-fast distinctions. Carried to its logical conclusion—which in practice it never was— the new scheme would mean suspension of the old system of rotating squadrons between active and quiet sectors. Rigidly applied, it would mean that, henceforth until the battle ended, squadrons in active sectors could expect no relief, while those in quiet ones would not be enjoying a well-earned rest but enduring relegation. To obviate such extremes, a class of squadrons intermediate in experience and fighting value between the most and the least distinguished, and capable of acting as occasional reliefs for the former, was introduced into the scheme. This arrangement fulfilled the purpose of a successful compromise by more or less restoring the status quo, so that everyone—or almost everyone—was satisfied.

After a quiet day on the 8th, Kesselring came again on September 9, this time with his striking-force significantly reduced by about a third. As on the 7th, the bombing was timed to begin about five o'clock, when workers on day shifts would be thinking of their evening meal, the six o'clock news, and the best way of getting through another night of the long-drawn danger and discomfort which Londoners had begun to take for granted.

On this day the defences came into their own after more than a week of doubt and stress. At half-past four, in face of growing indications that the Germans were massing across the Channel, Park posted a squadron over Canterbury. A quarter of an hour later he asked Brand to protect the aircraft factories west of London, and Leigh-Mallory his bases north of the Thames Estuary. By five o'clock he had nine of his own squadrons over Essex, Kent and Surrey.

Almost at that moment the first wave—about a hundred bombers, escorted and supported by fighters ahead, astern and on both flanks—crossed the coast near Dover and were promptly set upon by two of Park's squadrons sent forward for the purpose. A tremendous tussle between the fighters on both sides did not go all one way, but it settled the bombers' chances. Abandoning the hope of reaching London, they dropped most of their bomb-load on and round Canterbury and wheeled, with their close escort, over Sussex, where Park had three more squadrons ready to engage them.

The second wave, coming in at Beachy Head, were met soon after they crossed the coast by two squadrons which edged them westwards from the target-area, and were then engaged over south-west London by another of Park's squadrons and also by Leigh-Mallory's wing from Duxford. Almost as much disconcerted by the appearance of the Duxford wing over London as Park was by the desertion of his sector stations north of the river, the bombers scattered their bombs more or less aimlessly over a dozen boroughs and districts from Lambeth and Chelsea in the east to Kingston and Richmond in the west.

The outcome of the whole series of engagements was that fewer than half the bombers sent by Kesselring reached London; that hardly any of those which did get to London succeeded in bombing their intended targets; and that the Germans lost twenty-eight aircraft to Fighter Command's nineteen aircraft and fourteen pilots. With eighteen of the twenty-eight down on land or close off-shore, not even sceptical neutral journalists could deny that Dowding's pilots knew how to use their guns.

Although not usually regarded as one of the highlights of the battle, the action fought on September 9 was exceedingly important. Tactically it was, and is, extremely interesting as an almost classical example—marred only, from the textbook point of view, by the unrehearsed arrival of the Duxford wing—of the successful interception and engagement of two large and powerfully supported striking-forces by a small, compact, rigidly-controlled fighter force. But its importance was far more than tactical. Fighter Command's achievement made a profound impression on the Germans. Not surprisingly, the contrast between the Luftwaffe's success on the 7th and its failure on the 9th struck German observers very forcibly. On the 7th, more than three hundred bombers had been so ineffectively opposed before they dropped their bombs that practically all of them had reached not merely London, but the precise part of London where their objectives lay. On the 9th, the opposition was so strong that more than half the striking-force had no choice but to jettison its bombs or waste them on secondary targets, while most of the ninety bombers which did get somewhere near the target-area dropped theirs almost at random on residential districts. Undisputed air supremacy, the Naval War Staff noted, did not yet exist, although 'considerable fighter superiority' could be assumed.

Similarly, Hitler came to the conclusion on the 10th that the outcome of the air war still hung in the balance. He decided to postpone until the 14th the decision as to whether the preliminary order for invasion should be given or withheld. The delay would put back to the 24th—a better day with respect to moon and tide than the 21st—the earliest date on which troops could land, and might help to clarify the situation in the air. Thereupon Major-General Warlimont, Chief of the Operations Branch of the Supreme Headquarters Staff, handed Jodl the joint-service directive which it was intended to issue on the day when Hitler gave the preliminary order.

Except on the Supreme Headquarters front, the 10th was a quiet day. Not so the 11th. In the afternoon Kesselring made his third daylight attack on London since the 7th, this time sending only about a hundred bombers, most of which succeeded in reaching the neighbourhood of the City and the docks. At the same time a much smaller force attacked and badly damaged a brand-new aircraft factory near Southampton. Overestimating German losses, Dowding and his staff believed at the end of the day that the defences had done well. In fact, they had not only failed to interfere seriously with either raid but had lost more aircraft than the Luftwaffe.

The Germans did not make that mistake, although they, too, overestimated the enemy's losses. Several times during the next few days Hitler spoke highly of the work of Göring's airmen, describing it as 'above all praise'. On the 13th he told Brauchitsch and others in conversation that the chances of defeating Britain by air attack alone seemed so good that he had no thought of running the risks of an opposed landing.

This remark, which may have been inspired partly by doubts expressed by neutral commentators as to whether Londoners would stand up to repeated night attacks, was perhaps not very seriously meant. On a more formal occasion next day he drew the opposite conclusion, arguing that a successful landing was the quickest way of ending the war with Britain, and that nothing was lacking to make a landing possible except air superiority. But air superiority, he thought, was not far off. Struck by the uneven performance of the British air defences, he attributed it to the chances given to Dowding's squadrons to recover on quiet days when unfavourable weather prevented Göring from hammering home his advantage. All that was needed was a succession of fine days. Accordingly he would wait until the 17th to decide whether or not to issue the preliminary order for invasion, in the hope that the next few days would be fine and that Göring would get his chance.

This further postponement, announced in a characteristic harangue to his service advisers which began at three o'clock on September 14, meant that the earliest day on which troops could land in England was now the 27th. As the 27th was also the last day before October 8 on which the state of the tide would make a landing possible, and as postponement until October would mean that disembarkation could not be completed until winter was perilously near, it was obvious that the Luftwaffe had reached a crisis.

While Hitler and his service advisers were conferring in Berlin, Kesselring was making further attacks on London after quiet days on the 12th and 13th. Again, as on the 11th, the opposition was not very effective, and only fourteen German aircraft were shot down for the same number of Dowding's fighters lost.

That night victory must have seemed to Kesselring and Göring very near. The British, so unexpectedly strong on the 9th after their big but unsuccessful effort on the 7th, were clearly weakening. On the 11th, and again today, they had failed, as on the 7th, to save important targets from heavy bombing in broad daylight. So often in the past, as the Führer said, they had recovered when recovery seemed impossible; but this time, surely, they would not recover. If tomorrow was fine, one more supreme effort might bring the undisputed air superiority for which the Führer stipulated. At worst, its attainment could hardly be delayed beyond a day or two. If the Führer, satisfied that his airmen had the measure of the enemy, gave the preliminary order for invasion on the 17th, it was even possible that the British, worn out by further attacks by day and night, might decide to give up the unequal struggle by the time the troops were due to go ashore. And in that case the achievements of the Luftwaffe and its leaders would indeed be 'above all praise'.

II

The Climax

SUNDAY, SEPTEMBER 15, 1940—in some ways the most significant date in European history since Sunday, June 18, 1815—began as a cloudless autumn day with perfect visibility. In spite of the false alarm a week earlier, invasion was still expected almost hourly. On the 11th Winston Churchill had warned the public of preparations being made across the Channel, and had gone on to compare the situation with that existing when the Spanish Armada was approaching, or when Napoleon was waiting with his Grand Army at Boulogne. 'If this invasion is to be tried at all', he had said, 'it does not seem that it can be long delayed.'

At Park's sector stations and their forward aerodromes and satellites from the Sandlings to west Sussex, the pilots who would bear the burden of the daylight fighting were up early. At Debden and Martlesham on the borders of Suffolk and Essex, at North Weald in Epping Forest, at Hornchurch above Erith Reach, at Northolt and Hendon in the northern suburbs, at Croydon, Biggin Hill and Kenley, at Tangmere and Westhampnett below the hanging woods of Lavant Down, veterans of twenty-five who had survived a score of actions began to move at dawn from messes and billets to dispersal huts. Soon after breakfast the weather became less perfect, though still good. By the afternoon dense banks of cloud over parts of Kent and Essex were down to a few thousand feet.

Kesselring's plan for the great day was to use all his available bombers and fighters to make two attacks on London. With his bomber units cut to half their establishment by weeks of strain, he could not afford much in the way of feints or diversionary attacks, and his incurable shortage of fighters forced him to time his raids in such a way that some of his aircraft could take part in both. Thus there was no chance that the second raid would catch Park with his fighters rearming and refuelling after dealing with the first. Kesselring was, however, able to arrange with Sperrle for a few bombers diverted from the night offensive to attack Portland under cover of the second raid on London, and for the Messerschmitt 110s of his own fighter-bomber unit, Gruppe 210, to follow with a raid on the Supermarine factory at Eastleigh towards evening. These diversions could have no significant effect on the operations further east, but the first might catch Brand at an awkward moment when he was preoccupied with the situation on his left.

About half-past ten the first plots appeared on the operations table at Uxbridge. A few minutes later the Prime Minister and Mrs. Churchill, making a well-timed visit to Park's headquarters, were shown into the operations room.

As Kesselring's bombers and fighters gathered over the French coast under the all-seeing eye of the early-warning system, the vast, intricate machinery of interception went into action with impressive smoothness over thousands of square miles of southern England. In the group operations room far under the ground at Uxbridge, where even the great clock on the wall moved silently, hardly a sound rose above the faint hum of the ventilating mechanism. Brief orders quietly spoken into telephones, and repeated in sector and gun operations rooms from the Orwell and the Essex marshes to Selsey Bill, brought squadrons and guns to readiness. A few words exchanged between the controller and his opposite numbers at Rudloe and Watnall warned Nos. 10 and 12 Groups to be ready to reinforce. By the time the Germans had completed their ponderous assembly, British pilots were waiting in the cockpits of their aircraft at something like a dozen stations on a front from Cambridgeshire to Salisbury Plain.

The crossing of the Channel, too, seemed almost leisurely. At half-past eleven, when the German vanguard reached the English coast, Park had eleven of his twenty-one single-seater squadrons airborne, ten of them in pairs. On his right, the Spitfires of No. 609 (West Riding) Squadron were coming east from Middle Wallop to patrol the Windsor–Brooklands line; on his left the Duxford wing, five squadrons strong, was flying south towards North Weald, and was afterwards to veer south-west over London. To reach the target-area, the hundred-odd bombers and perhaps four hundred fighters Kesselring had sent would have to run the gauntlet of the five pairs of squadrons and one single squadron which Park was stringing along their route or close beside it, and would find the Duxford wing, with Bader leading, at the end of it.

The first squadrons ordered up, Nos. 72 and 92, were also the first in action. Both were crack squadrons, the first with what seemed a lifetime of struggle and survival behind them since their historic encounter with Stumpff's forlorn hope off the Farne Islands a month earlier; the second veterans of Dunkirk who had moved to Biggin Hill on the previous Sunday after a quiet spell at Pembrey. Somewhere near Canterbury they saw, ahead and to starboard, the puffs of smoke from anti-aircraft shells exploding in the wake of Kesselring's sprawling formation as it crossed the coast near Dover. As the range closed, German aircraft seemed to the twenty-four Spitfire pilots to stretch from horizon to horizon. But experience had taught them that skill, determination and a wary eye meant more than numbers, and that boldness paid. ('It was like rugger', said one fighter pilot. 'If you hesitated because you thought you might get hurt, you probably would get hurt.') Disregarding orders to take on the enemy's close escort because the only fighters visible were tucked away, absurdly, at the bottom of the formation, they plunged into the midst of the leading bombers, dodged Messerschmitt 109s which appeared from nowhere, and emerged from a desperate fight for life with many of their aircraft holed but with not a pilot hurt in either squadron. Almost simultaneously the Spitfires of No. 603 (City of Edinburgh) Squadron, who had shot down the first German aircraft of the war near the Forth Bridge in 1939, were attacking another part of the formation after flying more than fifty miles from their base at Hornchurch.

The three Spitfire squadrons were still in action when the first of the paired Hurricane squadrons joined the fight near Maidstone. At the best of times German fighter pilots had difficulty in staying with the bombers, especially on big days when a striking-force might include aircraft of three different types, each with its own limitations and all exasperatingly slow in the eyes of fighter pilots whose recurrent nightmare was an empty fuel-tank and a forced landing in the Channel. This morning was not the best of times. By the time the first five of Park's squadrons had made their contributions, Kesselring's armada was losing cohesion, and his fighter pilots were finding it harder than ever to know how to protect their charges as lame ducks dropped out of formation and stragglers fell behind.

Meanwhile Park had added six of his remaining ten single-seater squadrons to the two pairs of Hurricane squadrons coming towards the battle from stations north of the Thames. Among the squadrons approaching from north of the river was one, No. 257 Squadron, which had flown nearly sixty miles from Martlesham to its rendezvous at North Weald before turning south.

The Germans had hardly shaken off the attack at Maidstone when two of the squadrons last ordered up met them near the Medway towns and harried them for the next fifteen miles. More dispersed than ever, many with one or more of the crew killed or disabled, the surviving bombers continued over the south-eastern suburbs, still with German fighters scattered over a vast distance above and below them and on their flanks. There they were met by the four Hurricane squadrons from the northern sectors, and the air four miles over London was filled with a wheeling, seething mass of aircraft which left trails of white vapour in the September sky. With some of the Hurricanes diving on and through the bomber stream, while others scrapped fiercely with German fighters, the two sides were so inextricably confused that the Duxford wing, arriving at that moment, held off for a few minutes to get a clear run at their targets. By the time they were ready to attack, the centre of the vortex had shifted near enough to the target-area for crews to begin scattering their bombs, with little pretence at aiming, over London and its outskirts from Beckenham to Westminster. Houses in the crowded suburbs south of the Thames round New Cross and Lewisham suffered most, but two bridges and a small power-station were hit, and one bomb fell harmlessly in the grounds of Buckingham Palace, where a stick of bombs dropped on the 11th had already given the King the ordinary citizen's privilege of telling his own bomb story.

Before and after that day, the Duxford wing was fiercely criticised, not only on account of its reputation—hotly disclaimed by Leigh-Mallory—for arriving late, but on the ground that, like the German formations, it was unwieldy. Some opponents of the 'big wing' theory went so far as to allege that 'Bader's Balbo' was nothing but a propaganda stunt, a tacit criticism of Park's practice of using his squadrons singly or in pairs—and an unfair one, since the objectives Park had to defend were too near his bases for him to have time to assemble large formations. Leigh-Mallory's supporters retorted that the idea of defending objectives by interposing fighters between them and the enemy was fundamentally unsound; the right course was to leave the objectives in the care of their local anti-aircraft defences and concentrate on shooting down so many of the enemy's aircraft that he thought twice before he came again. Big wings, they said, meant light losses for one's own side and heavy losses for the enemy, and that was the whole art of air defence.

Apart from the difficulty of reconciling such an attitude with orders which Park had received to give fighter protection to specific objectives such as the aircraft factories at Brooklands, these arguments had at least one glaring weakness: there was no proof that big wings did mean light losses for one's own side and heavy losses for the enemy. If the losses of the Duxford wing were light, the obvious reason was that the remoteness of its starting-point prevented it from engaging the enemy except when he had already been engaged by Park's squadrons. As for the enemy's losses, there was not only no evidence that a five-squadron wing did shoot down more aircraft than five single squadrons would have done, but no reason why it should, unless the assumption that large wings frightened the enemy was a reason. For the truth was that a large wing was not really a tactical formation. Experience had shown that there was no place in air fighting, as it had developed since July, for the carefully-rehearsed formation attacks of peacetime exercises. Within a minute or two of going into action with a German formation which included fighters, a squadron was almost invariably forced to split up, preferably into pairs, as each pilot chose his target or was himself chosen as target by an opponent; and this applied as much when squadrons were massed in wings as when they were used singly. The cement that held the Duxford wing together was not the tactical superiority of massed squadrons but the invincible courage and determination of Douglas Bader.

For the German bomber crews the sight of Leigh-Mallory's fresh squadrons over London must nevertheless have been a dismal one. But the wing was not in the best position to engage, and was still climbing and manœuvring to get up-sun of the enemy when the bombers wheeled southwards, their bombs gone. A moment later German fighters dived on its leading squadrons, and their pilots, hardly waiting for Bader's order to 'weigh-in', were fighting for their lives in a furious dogfight which left the Poles of No. 310

40 *Messerschmitt 110 long-range fighters*

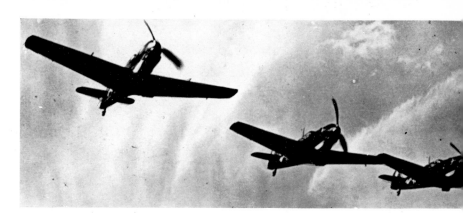

41 (above)   *Messerschmitt 109 short-range fighters*

42 (below)   *Junkers 87 dive-bombers*

GERMAN FIGHTERS
AND BOMBERS

43 (right)   *Junkers 88*

44 (centre)   *Heinkel 111*

45 (bottom)   *Dornier 17 bombers*

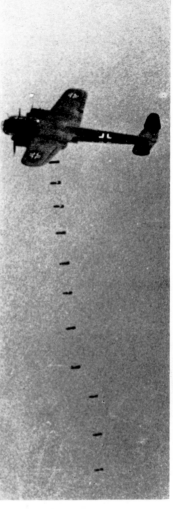

46 *Spitfire Mark I*

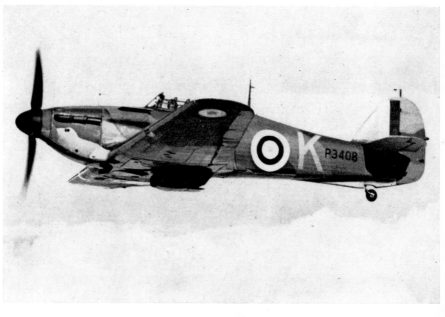

47 *A Hurricane of No. 85 squadron on patrol*

Squadron, eager to avenge their country's wrongs, with a clear run at the bombers and still together. At the cost of one pilot killed, another injured and four Hurricanes destroyed or damaged, they gave a good send-off to the retreating enemy.

As the German bombers and fighters streamed out over Kent and Sussex, Park put up his last four squadrons. The story goes that about this time Churchill asked Park or his controller how many squadrons he had left, received the answer 'None!' and, the report adds, 'looked grave'. A certain amount of confusion surrounds this incident, and some witnesses, confident that there was never a time when all No. 11 Group's Spitfire and Hurricane squadrons were in the air together, have denied that it can have taken place at all. The most probable explanation would seem to be that the first squadrons up had landed by the time the last were sent, and that, although not yet 'available' according to the indicator in the group operations room, they would have had at least a sporting chance of completing their rearming and refuelling in time to go up again if another attack—which Park was justified in assuming could only be a small one—had followed quickly.

As it was, Kesselring had nothing more he could risk sending before his own fighters were back, and there was time not only for Hurricanes and Spitfires to be refuelled and rearmed but for pilots to eat a hurried meal, and even for some who had landed away from their bases to return to them, before he came again.

Towards two o'clock plots began to build up again on the operations table. This time the warning was shorter; but it was long enough. Repeating his tactics of the morning but with even greater boldness, Park put up six pairs of squadrons while the leading German aircraft were still over the Channel, and added another two pairs and three and a half separate squadrons—all but a fraction of his remaining strength—as they crossed the coast. Again Brand patrolled the Windsor–Brooklands line, and again the Duxford wing came south.

Kesselring cannot have viewed with much satisfaction his arrangements for the second attack of the day as they emerged in their final form. Presumably because he had always meant to make the afternoon attack the heavier of the two, he had enough bombers to send a bigger bomb-load to London than had been dropped there in the morning; but his fighters would have been none too many to escort and support them even if all those with which he began the day had been available. As it was, with their effective strength reduced not only by the morning's losses but by the minor damage which always kept a good many aircraft on the ground immediately after a major operation, he was forced to stake a great deal on the success of an advanced guard of high-flying, freelance fighters whose orders were to clear the sky over London of Hurricanes and Spitfires. On the other hand, the gathering clouds would make it—and did make it—more difficult for the Observer Corps to keep track of incoming formations and assess their strength, and hence more difficult for Park's subordinates to position fighters so unerringly as to make sure that no part of Kesselring's array was missed before it reached the target-area. For this reason, the British control system did not work with quite the clockwork precision which had made the morning's effort like a controller's dream come true.

Making the most of the weather factor, either designedly or simply because conditions were not good enough for a dense swarm of bombers and fighters to stay together, the bombers and their close escort crossed the coast of Kent in two formations, with the advanced guard above and drawing ahead of them. Much as in the morning, one formation was intercepted near Canterbury, this time by a pair of squadrons from Hornchurch, and again near Maidstone, but by half a squadron only. Further west, a pair of squadrons from Tangmere met Kesselring's left wing near Edenbridge, attacked it, and forced some of the bombers to jettison their bombs and turn for home. The rest, not very effectively escorted, continued towards London.

This formation, too, was to be intercepted a second time before it reached the target-area. Flying towards it across London in the Hurricane earmarked for his own use was Group-Captain S. F. Vincent, commanding the Northolt sector. A big, burly man, long past the normal age for a fighter pilot, Vincent had no thought of doing more than see for himself how his squadrons were faring and how things were going. South of London he was startled to see a formidable number of German bombers flying steadily towards him as if on a peacetime demonstration flight, with not a British fighter in sight and with their escort taking no apparent interest in their welfare or in him. A good-natured man who viewed human imperfections with the genial tolerance which often goes with a large frame, he nevertheless felt that this time the Germans had gone too far and that some protest must be made. He made it. He must have been astonished, and was certainly delighted, when the sequel to his head-on attack was that some of the leading bombers fell out of formation and turned away.

Meanwhile Kesselring's advanced guard had reached the neighbourhood of Dartford with little or no opposition. A tremendous fighter-to-fighter battle, with the greater part of fifteen British squadrons going into action over a period of well under half an hour with approximately equal or slightly inferior numbers, followed over the south-eastern suburbs. The all-out tussle with the British fighter force which was to have brought the Germans undisputed air superiority had come at last; and its outcome was a bitter disappointment to Kesselring's fighter pilots. In spite of all they had been told, they found Dowding's squadrons apparently stronger than ever, and could make no impression on them. 'I had a ten-minute fight, without success', wrote Adolf Galland, the leading exponent of the freelance fighter sweep, 'and ten minutes is a long time in air fighting.' The most the German fighter force could claim—and it might have been enough if air superiority had not been the object— was that they held their own and that the fighter battle did give a good many of the bombers a clear run at their targets. Although nothing like as destructive as the first big raid on the 7th, the attack did a fair amount of damage on both banks of the river, and several public utility undertakings were hit.

Not all combats over London were with fighters. The Duxford wing, arriving when the fighter-to-fighter battle was past its peak, saw bombers 'scattered about in all sorts of formations all over the sky', and many of its pilots, notably the Poles of No. 310 Squadron and the Czechs of No. 302, attacked them ruthlessly in ones and twos after the wing had split up in a dogfight with Messerschmitt 109s. One Polish pilot pushed his attack on a blazing Dornier 17 so relentlessly, and to such close quarters, that he collided with one of the crew who was baling out, and afterwards made a forced landing with his airscrew smashed and his engine-cowling stained with blood. Although few encounters were as gruesome, the incident was only one of many which helped to thin the ranks of bomber crews so drastically that September 15 was long remembered as a day of terror in the German bomber force.

The raid on Portland by Sperrle's handful of unescorted bombers caught Brand, according to plan, with two of his three Spitfire squadrons from Middle Wallop reinforcing Park. In spite of half an hour's warning, the remaining squadron reached the bombers only when they were retreating; but the attack did little damage. Gruppe 210, following about three hours after the climax over London, were equally successful and their performance was even more spectacularly ineffective. Reaching Eastleigh without fighter opposition although Park and Brand were able to put four squadrons into the air before their arrival and a fifth later, they gave a superb display of formation flying in the teeth of anti-aircraft fire, missed the target from two thousand feet, and were off like lightning. In any case these gestures, successful or unsuccessful, could not alter a line of the sentence of dismissal passed on Göring's hopes by the decisive battle over London.

On reflection, German fighter pilots were not dissatisfied with their performance on September 15. They had met the enemy in fair fight, they had fought well, and their losses were not excessive. After seeing Dowding put a hundred and eighty fighters over London in one brief but highly significant encounter, and twice in one day put three hundred or more over the south-eastern counties in an hour and a half, they were, however, more than ever dissatisfied with superiors who had repeatedly told them that he had only a hundred aircraft left. Even Göring, who could not deny that Dowding was still very strong and that the figures produced by the intelligence branch were nonsense, continued for a day or two to assert that four or five days of heavy fighting ought to see the end of him, although 'it will never be possible to prevent fighters from appearing repeatedly here and there'. But bomber units told a different story. Measured by the number of aircraft written off, their casualties were not prohibitive: bombers and fighters together, the Luftwaffe had lost sixty aircraft on September 15, and not all these losses were attributable to British guns and fighters. But this figure said nothing of the number of bombers which had landed with one or more of the crew dead or wounded, or so badly shot up that their arrival on the right side of the Channel seemed a miracle. To survivors of blood-curdling encounters with British and Czech and Polish pilots, to men who had seen and heard and felt what Dowding's supposedly exhausted fighter force could do between the coast and London to bombers escorted and supported by every fighter Kesselring could muster, it was obvious that he and they had taken a desperate beating. Had bomber crews been present when Göring spoke glibly to Kesselring and Sperrle on the 16th of further attacks by three or four hundred bombers at a time 'in perfect weather', his words would have seemed to them the vapourings of a mountebank.

At any rate there was one thing on which all could agree. Whether Göring was right or wrong in thinking air superiority attainable, it had not been attained. What was more, its attainment seemed further off than ever; certainly much further off than it had looked two days earlier. To senior officers acquainted with the Supreme Command's time-table it was obvious that, in any case, speculations as to what four or five fine days might bring were academic, because there were not four or five days left.

The weather on the 16th was indifferent. Kesselring undertook no major operations, and was probably in no state to undertake any even if the weather had been good. On the 17th the Führer, agreeing with the Naval Staff that the Royal Air Force was 'still by no means defeated', and noting that a period of 'turbulent wind conditions' was expected rather than the flat calm needed for a landing, decided not to issue the preliminary invasion order and postponed the operation 'until further notice'. Next day, informed through Jodl that the effects on the invasion fleet of British air and naval bombardment were becoming serious, he ordered that no more shipping should be assembled in the Channel ports and agreed that naval and transport vessels should be dispersed. Although the fiction that the project might be revived was kept up for some time, effectively the spectre of German domination of the civilised world through the elimination of Germany's last enemy in Western Europe by invasion had been laid as the outcome of Göring's all-out struggle with the British fighter force.

I2

The Anticlimax

LOGICALLY, the Battle of Britain ought to have ended at nightfall on September 15, when Kesselring's bomber crews were counting their losses and drowning their sorrows in Schnapps. Once Göring's attempt to gain air superiority in time for invasion had failed, as clearly it had, his obviously right course was to revert whole-heartedly to the policy of blockade. Had he made up his mind at once to devote his bomber force entirely to attacks on shipping, at the same time improving and strengthening its offshoot which shadowed ocean convoys for the benefit of Raeder's submarines, the Battle of the Atlantic would have begun some weeks before it did, and the Germans would at any rate have been that much nearer to success.

But that course would have left the short-range fighter force in France with little to do for as long as the British found it expedient to keep their Channel convoys out of range in daylight. Moreover, Göring was determined to persevere with his attempt to hasten the effects of blockade by making life uncomfortable for Londoners. At the same time he was reluctant to give up hope that Dowding might yet be worn down by a combination of bombing and air combat. He therefore ordered not only that night bombing of London should continue but that 'harassing attacks' should be made in daylight. At the same time, further attempts would be made to destroy aircraft factories.

Nominally, 'repeated attacks in perfect weather with three to four hundred bombers' continued to figure in the programme; but these were obviously impractical, not only because the weather after the middle of September was seldom perfect but also because the means of making them did not exist. To send four hundred bombers to London in daylight with any prospect of winning an accompanying fighter battle, Kesselring would have needed not only the four

154

hundred bombers—themselves hard enough to find without pre-
judicing the night offensive—but also at least eight hundred short-
range fighters to go with them. How far he was from commanding
such resources was shown on September 18, when he made his first
daylight raid on London since the 15th. In spite of the two days'
rest, he mustered only about seventy bombers, and found the going
very hard in spite of a numerically sufficient fighter escort.

On the other hand, Sperrle succeeded in pushing home a number
of damaging attacks on aircraft factories. On September 25 about
sixty of his bombers, escorted by long-range fighters, attacked the
Bristol Aeroplane Company's factory and one of Brand's sector
stations, both at Filton, under cover of a diversionary attack on
Portland. No. 10 Group, assuming that the main force was bound
for the Westland factory at Yeovil, which was known to figure in
the German target-list, began by sending their fighters in the wrong
direction, and only a few pilots caught up with the bombers before
they reached the target. Next day Dowding made one of his rare
tactical interventions, sending a squadron of Hurricanes from
Park's group to Filton to guard against a repetition. Either exceptionally well informed from an inside source or a first-class guesser,
he was soon proved to have acted wisely. Within twenty-four hours
the attack he expected was delivered, and the reinforcing squadron
met the bombers on their inward route and forced them to jettison
their bombs.

Three days later the long-awaited attack on the Westland factory
came at last. It found the defences more than ready. Intercepted by
at least four squadrons on the way in and by four more in the
neighbourhood of Yeovil, and hampered by dense clouds, Sperrle's
bombers missed the target.

Throughout the autumn and early winter, Kesselring met Göring's
demand for harassing attacks by sending fighters across the Channel
at heights which gave the Messerschmitt 109 a clear advantage over
the versions of the Hurricane and Spitfire with which most of
Park's squadrons were equipped. Had Park been sure that Kesselring's high-fliers were all fighters pure and simple, he could have
afforded to ignore them; but Kesselring forestalled him by fitting
some of his fighters with external bomb-racks, and by including an
occasional Junkers 88 in his formations. In consequence Park had
no choice but to intercept them, and at times was even driven to the

desperate expedient of putting standing patrols over Kent to make sure that they were not missed. Thus the high-flying sweeps did harass Park, inasmuch as they cost him a good many wasted sorties; but they brought Kesselring no decision in his favour, and could bring him none.

Faced afterwards with the need to choose an arbitrary date on which the battle could be reckoned to have ended for statistical and administrative purposes, the Air Ministry drew the line on the last day of October. The date was well chosen, inasmuch as Göring reverted to blockade next day by devoting some of Kesselring's effort to attacks on shipping in the Thames Estuary. On the other hand, the attacks were similar in many ways to those with which the preliminary phase had opened in July, so that they might, with equal logic, have been included in the battle.

By any definition, the battle was on its last legs when the Italian Air Force made their belated contribution. With no encouragement from Hitler, Mussolini had insisted that an Italian contingent should travel to Belgium to claim its share of glory. By the time of its arrival, Göring had thrown away the chance of victory; but it was not for Mussolini's pilots to reason why.

On the night of October 25, sixteen Italian bombers, attacking Harwich, made the first of a series of night attacks on east coast towns which continued well into the early winter. By the time the night offensive ended early in January, the Italian bomber force had flown between seventy and eighty night sorties, had dropped about forty-five tons of bombs, and had lost no aircraft to the defences although at least one bomber had crashed on take-off. According to German and Italian records, the targets attacked at night were Harwich, Ipswich, Lowestoft and Yarmouth; but whether bombs were aimed at built-up areas in general, or at supposed military objectives, the published record does not show.

On October 29 fifteen Italian bombers, liberally escorted and supported by more than seventy Italian fighters, set out in daylight to attack an objective near Ramsgate, perhaps Manston aerodrome. Both bombers and fighters were engaged by anti-aircraft fire, presumably from the Manston aerodrome defences or the Thames and Medway guns; but either the gunners did not identify the attackers as Italian, or were not believed, for their nationality does not seem to have been suspected by any authoritative British annalist until the war was over and German and Italian records were available.

Just under a fortnight later, on Armistice Day, pilots of two Hurricane squadrons put up to intercept a raid approaching the Thames Estuary were amazed to meet forty Fiat C.R. 42 fighters escorting ten Italian bombers afterwards found to be bound for Harwich and its shipping. The Italian fighter pilots fought gallantly and the bombers held their formation and put up the best defence they could. But the C.R. 42, a biplane, was hopelessly outclassed by the Hurricane, and the Italians lost three bombers and three fighters without shooting down a single British aircraft.

After this experience the Italians made no more daylight raids on objectives in Great Britain or British waters. But their fighters continued to make offensive sweeps. On November 23 twenty-nine C.R. 42s had a final encounter with British fighters and lost two aircraft. All told, the Italian contingent in Belgium flew more than seventeen hundred offensive and defensive sorties between October, 1940, and April, 1941, and the lives of twenty pilots and other aircrew were sacrificed to Mussolini's ambition to claim a share in the destruction of the Royal Air Force.

The Italian contribution, pathetic yet not contemptible, ill-fated but courageous, was a fitting postscript to an attempt which began with high hopes and in fine summer weather, and which fizzled out in drenching rain and choking fog and seething disappointment. Except from the uncompromising viewpoint of the statistician and the bestower of honours, mentions and rewards, the German effort and the British counter-effort did not end abruptly, but tailed off as fine days became rarer and bad days more prohibitive. Yet somewhere a farewell must be made, the curtain dropped, the story ended. All things considered, perhaps the fittest point is that at which the leading actor left the scene.

On November 25, 1940, Air Chief Marshal Dowding was succeeded by Air Marshal W. S. Douglas (afterwards Marshal of the Royal Air Force Lord Douglas of Kirtleside). With the night bomber still undefeated, and likely to remain so until more and better radar for guns and fighters was forthcoming, the architect of victory in the all-important daylight battle slipped out almost as quietly as he had come. The once-handsome grounds of Bentley

Priory were cluttered now with huts and offices. The basement still smelled damp. The view from the terrace beyond the drawing-room was still superb. The place was more populous, but not more important, than on that fine midsummer day four years before when he first set eyes on it, and when war seemed so immeasurably far away to everyone but him and a few who shared his knowledge and his foresight.

At that point the curtain falls on a contest unique in history and on its leading figure—the only man who ever won a major fighter battle or will ever win one. For such encounters between massed aircraft on both sides are gone for ever with the advent of the nuclear bomb, the global bomber and the ballistic missile.

Chronology

1922

Responsibility for air defence of Great Britain transferred from War Office to Air Ministry. War Office to continue to provide and man anti-aircraft guns and searchlights.

British Government adopt scheme for metropolitan air force of 14 bomber and 9 fighter squadrons.

1923

British Government adopt scheme for metropolitan air force of 35 bomber and 17 fighter squadrons, to be completed at end of 1928 or later.

1925

British Government postpone completion of air expansion scheme until 1936 in view of better international outlook.

1929

British Government postpone completion of air expansion scheme until 1938 in view of impending world economic crisis.

1931

Spring. Field-Marshal Sir George Milne, Chief of Imperial General Staff, warns Committee of Imperial Defence of emergence of Rome-Berlin Axis.

Summer. British Government reaffirm long-standing assumption that there will be no major war involving the British Empire for at least ten years.

Autumn. Japanese invasion of Manchuria brings risk of major war in Far East.

1932

Japanese attack Shanghai. Great Britain and United States powerless to protect Far Eastern interests except at cost of major war in which initial advantage would lie with Japan.

Chiefs of Staff call on British Government to cancel ten-year rule and provide for purely defensive commitments.

Government cancel ten-year rule, but continue to hope that Disarmament Conference at Geneva will lead to abolition or limitation of air warfare.

1933

November. Facing breakdown at Geneva, British Government appoint Defence Requirements Committee to advise on measures to repair worst deficiencies in national defences.

1934

February. Defence Requirements Committee report that Germany, dominated for past year and more by Adolf Hitler, is 'ultimate potential enemy', and may be ready for war in 1938 or 1939. They advocate 'balanced strategy', to include putting of United Kingdom in 'thoroughly defensible condition' and preparation of Expeditionary Force for despatch to Low Countries in event of war, partly for purpose of keeping German bomber force at arm's length.

July. British Government reject plea for balanced strategy, and adopt scheme for metropolitan air force of 43 bomber and 28 fighter squadrons in hope that threat of air expansion will induce Hitler to modify his aims.

November–December. In view of inability of system based on sound-locators and acoustic mirrors to give timely warning of approach of fast-moving modern bombers, H. E. Wimperis, Director of Scientific Research, Air Ministry, suggests creation of Committee for Scientific Survey of Air Defence under H. T. Tizard, Chairman of Aeronautical Research Committee, to seek new approach to problem. Air Chief Marshal Sir Robert Brooke-Popham, commanding Air Defence of Great Britain and Chairman of committee appointed to study re-orientation of air defences to meet threat from Germany, also calls attention to defects of existing system. Others aware of need for new devices include Winston Churchill and Professor F. A. Lindemann.

1935

January. Wimperis consults R. A. Watson-Watt of National Physical Laboratory about possibility of using electro-magnetic radiations to harm hostile aircraft or their occupants. Watson-Watt declares proposal impractical, but suggests detection and location of approaching aircraft by means known afterwards as R.D.F. and ultimately as radar.

Committee for Scientific Survey of Air Defence hold first meeting on 28th, invite Watson-Watt to follow up idea, and arrange that Air Chief Marshal Sir Hugh Dowding, Air Member for Research and Development, shall be asked to seek sanction for expenditure on project.

February 26. Watson-Watt demonstrates new method at Weedon for Dowding's benefit.

March–June. Dowding asks for, and obtains, substantial financial backing. Experimental station set up at Orfordness.

Sir John Simon, Foreign Secretary, and Anthony Eden, Minister for League of Nations Affairs, told (incorrectly) by Hitler that Luftwaffe is already as strong as Royal Air Force. British Government adopt scheme for metropolitan air force of 70 bomber and 35 fighter squadrons.

July–December. Air Ministry adopt radar as basis of early-warning system. Work on acoustic mirrors stopped. 6 radar stations to be built immediately as first instalment of about 20 intended to cover coast from Tyne to Southampton.

Tense relations with Italy, arising from Abyssinian War, lead to despatch to Alexandria and Malta of most of material earmarked for home defence in event of war. United Kingdom virtually defencelsss against local attack.

1936

February. British Government adopt new scheme of air expansion which, unlike predecessors, makes good provision for reserves. Metropolitan air force to include 70 bomber and 30 fighter squadrons by March, 1939. Hurricane and Spitfire, under development since 1934, to replace existing fighters. Shadow factories organised by motor-car manufacturers to supplement efforts of aircraft industry.

July 14. Command and control of air defences divorced from command of metropolitan bomber force. Post of Air Officer Commanding-in-Chief, Air Defence of Great Britain, abolished. Fighter Command formed to undertake air defence of United Kingdom. Air Chief Marshal Sir Hugh Dowding assumes command of fighters and barrage-balloons, and control of anti-aircraft guns and searchlights.

October 1. Luftwaffe known in London to have reached first-line strength of roughly 1,100 aircraft. Expected to rise to 1,500 aircraft in spring of 1937, and ultimately to not less than 4,000 aircraft. First-line strength of British metropolitan air force 696 aircraft; due to rise to 1,736 aircraft in spring of 1939.

1937

February. Committee of experts under Dowding, invited to draw up 'ideal' scheme of air defence on assumption that problems of supply can be disregarded, recommend provision of 45 fighter squadrons, 1,264 anti-aircraft guns and 4,700 searchlights, in addition to light anti-aircraft weapons and balloons for protection against low-level attack.

Summer. Committee of Imperial Defence approve 'ideal' scheme of air defence in principle.

1938

Spring. Germans seize Austria.

British Government abandon rule that rearmament must not interfere with normal trade, authorise Air Ministry to order up to 12,000 aircraft, and adopt new air expansion scheme. Metropolitan air force to include 73 bomber and 38 fighter squadrons by spring of 1940.

Sir Kingsley Wood succeeds Lord Swinton as Secretary of State for Air (May 16).

Autumn. Munich crisis. Of 29 fighter squadrons reckoned mobilisable, only 5 have modern aircraft. No stored reserves of fighters. Radar chain and communications incomplete. London balloon-barrage deploys 142 balloons towards establishment of 450. About one-third of required number of anti-aircraft guns and searchlights available, but most guns obsolete or obsolescent and some not in working order.

On advice of Sir Thomas Inskip, Minister for Co-ordination of Defence, Sir Kingsley Wood rules that fighters shall have first claim on aircraft industry.

November. Air Ministry adopt scheme for expansion of metropolitan air force to 85 bomber and 50 fighter squadrons by 1942.

1939

Spring. Germans seize Bohemia and Moravia in defiance of Munich Agreement.

British Government sanction definitive staff talks with French.

British and French staffs agree that 4 British fighter squadrons shall go to France on outbreak of war to support army in the field; position to be reviewed if no heavy air attacks made on United Kingdom in first six months. Home defence establishment after deduction of the 4 squadrons fixed at 53 fighter squadrons, 1,450 balloons, 2,232 heavy anti-aircraft guns, 1,860 light anti-aircraft barrels, 4,128 searchlights.

Summer. Radar chain brought into operation. Dowding authorised to intercept unauthorised flights over United Kingdom. German aircraft reconnoitre over North Sea and English Channel, but do not infringe territorial limits.

August 23. Germany signs pact with Russia.

September 1. German troops invade Poland.

September 3. Britain declares war on Germany.
    Four British fighter squadrons ordered to France.
    Strength of home air defences 35 fighter squadrons (of which 6 obsolete or obsolescent), 624 balloons, 695 heavy anti-aircraft guns (270 obsolescent), 253 light anti-aircraft barrels, 2,700 searchlights.

September 16. Dowding protests against despatch of 4 squadrons while home air defences still weak, and warns Air Ministry against allowing output of modern fighters to be drained away in France.

December 18. Fighter force reaches planned figure of 57 squadrons. Two more squadrons have gone to France, leaving 51 at home, of which about a third not yet fit for active service.

1940

February–March. Dowding asks Air Staff to review needs of home defence.
    Air Commodore D. F. Stevenson, Director of Home Operations, recommends immediate formation of 7 additional fighter squadrons, but output and reserves are insufficient. In late February only 16 Hurricanes and Spitfires ready for immediate issue from stored reserves; output of single-seater fighters for whole month 143.

April 9. Germans invade Denmark and Norway.

May 8. Air Ministry sanction formation of 3 additional fighter squadrons.

May 10. Criticism of British Government's handling of Norwegian campaign leads to resignation of Neville Chamberlain and replacement as Prime Minister by Winston Churchill. New Government's plans include creation of Ministry of Aircraft Production under Lord Beaverbrook.
    Germans invade France and the Low Countries.
    Air Ministry order 4 more fighter squadrons to France. Strength at home reduced to 43 fit squadrons, of which 2 earmarked for Norway.

May 13. Air Ministry order equivalent of 2 more fighter squadrons to France. More than half initial equipment of fighter squadrons in France already lost.

May 14. German troops cross Meuse in Ardennes sector. M. Reynaud, French Premier, asks British Government for 10 more fighter squadrons.

May 15. Dowding attends meeting of War Cabinet at own request and warns ministers that compliance with French request will rule out successful defence of United Kingdom. War Cabinet decide not to send the 10 squadrons.

May 16. War Cabinet revert to earlier decision to send another 8 half-squadrons. Strength at home reduced to equivalent of 36 or 37 squadrons.
    Dowding warns Air Council that any further weakening of his command will entail 'final, complete and irremediable defeat'.

May 18. Germans drive wedge between Franco–British forces north of the Somme and those south of it.

May 19. General Pownall, Chief of Staff to Field-Marshal Gort, commanding British Expeditionary Force, warns War Office that attempt may have to be made to withdraw force under pressure. Loss of up to four-fifths of force thought probable.
    Prime Minister rules that no more fighter squadrons shall go to France in any circumstances.

May 20. Germans reach Channel coast. Hitler 'beside himself with joy'.

May 21. Grand-Admiral Raeder, Commander-in-Chief of German Navy, asks Hitler whether he means to put troops ashore in England. Hitler reaffirms policy of starving Britain out by naval and air blockade if she fails to make peace of her own accord.

May 26–June 4. Bulk of British Expeditionary Force successfully withdrawn by way of Dunkirk, but practically all heavy equipment left behind. Intermittent fighter cover by part of Dowding's force under Air Vice-Marshal Park brings destruction of 132 German aircraft for loss of 80 British fighter pilots.
    British Chiefs of Staff advise Government that Britain's ability to carry on war alone if France falls will depend primarily on supply of fighters.
    Output of Hurricanes and Spitfires exceeds estimate for May by 23 per cent.

June 14. Germans enter Paris.

June 16. Reynaud proposes to carry on war from North Africa, falls from power, and is replaced by Pétain.

June 18. Count Ciano, Italian Foreign Minister, learns that Germany has made peace-offer to Britain through Swedish Legation in Berlin.

June 22. French sign armistice with Germany. Great Britain sole opponent of Germany still at war.

June 29–30. Hitler completes tour of occupied France and Belgium, returns to Germany, and is shown memorandum advocating intensified air attacks on Britain, to be followed 'if necessary' by a landing in August or September.

Output of Hurricanes and Spitfires exceeds estimate for June by 53 per cent.

July 2. Hitler orders armed forces to make provisional plans for invasion of Britain.

Reich Marshal Göring, German Air Minister and Commander-in-Chief of Luftwaffe, orders intensified air blockade of Britain, with special emphasis on attacks on shipping by Luftflotten 2 (Field-Marshal Kesselring) and 3 (Field-Marshal Sperrle).

July 4. Sperrle successfully attacks ocean convoy outward-bound off Portland.

British Admiralty accelerate plans for diversion of ocean traffic to west coast ports.

July 7. Ciano sees Hitler in Berlin and finds him 'rather inclined to unleash a storm of wrath and steel on the British'.

July 10. Kesselring, attacking coastal convoy in Straits of Dover, loses 3 or more aircraft in brisk skirmish with Park's fighters. Beginning of Battle of Britain (preliminary phase) according to British reckoning.

July 11–24. Further attacks by Kesselring and Sperrle on coastal convoys. Dowding responds cautiously in view of probable major attacks on United Kingdom. Germans lose 93 aircraft between 10th and 24th, Fighter Command 48 aircraft.

July 11. Raeder tells Hitler that he regards invasion of Britain as 'last resort'.

July 13. Field-Marshal von Brauchitsch, Commander-in-Chief of German Army, and General Halder, his Chief of Staff, submit ambitious proposals for invasion of Britain. Hitler orders them to begin active preparations.

July 16. Hitler formally instructs armed forces to prepare for invasion of Britain. Attainment of air superiority indispensable prelude to a landing.

July 17. Brauchitsch orders 13 picked divisions to Channel coast as first wave of landing-force.

July 19. Hitler makes 'last appeal for peace' in speech to Reichstag.

July 21. Hitler tells service chiefs that Britain's position is 'hopeless', and orders General Staff to make preliminary studies for an attack on Russia.

July 22. British Government reject German peace-offer.

July 25. Kesselring attacks coastal convoy in Straits of Dover after shadowing it from Thames Estuary. German light surface craft are driven off by destroyers, but return at night. 11 ships out of 21 sunk or badly damaged.

July 26. British Admiralty suspend merchant traffic through Straits in daylight.

July 27. Kesselring sinks 2 destroyers and damages a third.

July 28. Destroyers of Dover Command withdrawn to Portsmouth.

July 29. Sperrle sinks a destroyer. Eastern half of Channel closed to British destroyers in daylight, but minesweepers continue to keep searched channels open.

July 30. Hitler warns Göring to be ready to begin 'the great air battle against England' at twelve hours' notice. Göring's plans not yet complete.

July 31. Output of Hurricanes and Spitfires exceeds estimate for July by 51 per cent. More than 1,200 delivered since May 1.

August 2. Göring issues Battle of Britain directive. Attacks on objectives in south of England by Kesselring and Sperrle to be concerted after first day with attacks on objectives in north and Midlands by Luftflotte 5 (General Stumpff). Collapse of air defences in south expected within four days, of Royal Air Force as a whole within four weeks.

August 5. First Channel convoy since July 23 leaves Falmouth; ultimately reaches Thames Estuary safely by lying up in daylight.

August 6. Göring orders Kesselring and Sperrle to begin operations on August 10 (*Adler-Tag*) in accordance with his directive of August 2.

August 7–8. First west-bound Channel convoy since July 25 leaves Thames Estuary at dusk, is detected by German radar, ambushed by light surface craft, and attacked by aircraft. Many ships hit by bombs or gunfire and at least seven sunk.

August 10. Adler-Tag postponed in view of unfavourable weather forecasts.

August 12. Preliminary phase of battle ends with attacks on British aerodromes and radar stations in preparation for main offensive. Destruction of 286 German aircraft and 150 British fighters since July 10 has left relative first-line strengths practically unchanged, but manufacture of 500 Hurricanes and Spitfires has enabled British to build up stored reserves.

August 13. Adler-Tag. Kesselring and Sperrle fly nearly 500 bomber and 1,000 fighter sorties; Fighter Command 700 sorties. Cloudy weather, last-minute misunderstandings and unexpectedly strong opposition result in sharp set-back for Luftwaffe. Germans lose 45 aircraft, Fighter Command 13 aircraft but only 7 pilots.

August 14. Second day's operations postponed in view of weather forecast.

August 15. Second day of major operations. Luftwaffe fly 1,786 sorties, Fighter Command 974. Stumpff attacks across North Sea from Denmark and Norway and is decisively repulsed with loss of one-sixth of his force. British suffer damage to several aerodromes and lose 34 fighters, but end day with 235 Hurricanes and Spitfires in stored reserves after all wastage has been made good. Germans lose 75 aircraft all told.

Göring initiates triangular dispute between High Command and bomber and fighter leaders by insisting on stronger close escort for bombers.

August 16. Third day of major operations. Luftwaffe fly 1,715 sorties, Fighter Command 776. Germans lose 45 aircraft. British suffer considerable damage to aerodromes and lose 21 fighters in the air and a number of aircraft on the ground.

August 17. Luftwaffe make no major attacks, although weather not prohibitive.

British Air Ministry sanction stop-gap measures to alleviate threatened shortage of fighter pilots.

August 18. Fourth day of major operations emphasizes German failure to eliminate air defences of southern England within time allotted. Luftwaffe lose 71 aircraft to Fighter Command's 27, bringing totals for four days to 236 and 95 respectively.

First phase of main offensive ends with Germans dissatisfied with lack of progress and heavy bomber losses. British have 161 Hurricanes and Spitfires in stored reserves, but no reserve of fully-trained pilots outside squadrons.

August 19. Göring issues orders for next phase. Renewed emphasis on destruction of British fighter force as first step to success. Striking forces for major operations by day to be limited to numbers for which strong escort and support can be provided. Kesselring to shoulder main burden in daylight, with object of tempting Dowding to commit best part of his force against superior numbers of German fighters. Sperrle to back him, largely by attacking aircraft factories at night or with cloud cover, and to plan night attack on Liverpool. Stumpff to plan night attack on Glasgow.

August 24. After five days of indifferent weather, Kesselring opens new phase with attacks on aerodrome in Kent and Essex. Park, commanding under Dowding in southern England, responds energetically, but his pilots find strongly-supported German bombers hard to reach. Sperrle attacks Portsmouth, many crews missing dockyard but hitting town. Luftwaffe lose 38 aircraft, Fighter Command 22.

At night, bomber crews sent to attack aircraft factories and other objectives drop bombs on London against orders. London's first experience of bombing since 1918.

August 25. Sperrle sends 45 bombers with more than 200 fighters to attack fighter aerodrome in Dorset. Air Vice-Marshal Brand, commanding in south-west, puts up strong defence and is reinforced by Park, but German fighters are so numerous that air defences destroy only 1 bomber (and 11 fighters) for loss of 11 of their own aircraft and 8 pilots. Aerodrome badly damaged. German losses for whole day 20 aircraft, British 16.

At night, Germans attack objectives at Birmingham and elsewhere. British, not knowing that bombing of London on 24th was unintentional, send bombers to Berlin.

August 26. Kesselring attempts attacks on aerodromes in Kent, Essex and Suffolk with only partial success; Sperrle makes ineffective attack on Portsmouth and is roughly handled by defences. One of Park's aerodromes badly damaged, but German bomber force suffers fairly heavily for first time since August 18. Luftwaffe lose 41 aircraft, Fighter Command 31.

Fortnight expires during which Hitler was to decide whether progress of air offensive justifies completion of invasion programme, but he reaches no decision.

August 28. Kesselring renews attacks on aerodromes after quiet day on 27th. In afternoon, sends fighters without bombers, and successfully tempts Park to an unprofitable exchange of casualties on a minor scale, each side losing about 9 aircraft. Luftwaffe lose 30 aircraft all told, Fighter Command 20.

At night, Sperrle makes first of four successive night attacks on Liverpool. Loses only 7 bombers in more than 600 sorties, but achieves no tactical or strategic gain. Air defences almost powerless without special equipment still in experimental stage.

August 29. Kesselring makes more fighter sweeps but no major attacks. Luftwaffe lose 17 aircraft, Fighter Command 9.

General von Döring, chief of Kesselring's fighter organisation, claims that 'unlimited fighter superiority' has been attained.

August 30. Fighter Command, supposed by Germans to have only a few hundred aircraft left, fly more than 1,000 daylight sorties for first time. Kesselring attacks aerodromes in Kent and aircraft factory at Luton. Heavy damage at Biggin Hill (fighter sector station) and Luton. Luftwaffe lose 36 aircraft, Fighter Command 26.

Hitler announces that he will decide on or about September 10 whether to give or withhold preliminary order for invasion. If decision favourable, troops will sail on September 20, and land on 21st between Folkestone and New Romney, Camber and Eastbourne, and Birling Gap and Brighton. First objective line Brighton–Uckfield–Tenterden–Ashford–Canterbury.

He expresses wish to make concentrated attacks on London as reprisals for bombing of Berlin.

August 31–September 6. Kesselring continues bombing of aerodromes and also attacks aircraft factories and oil refineries, but scale of attack falls off after maximum effort on August 31. Park suffers crippling damage to sector stations, but avoids all-out fighter-to-fighter battle on Kesselring's terms and preserves his force substantially intact through week of crisis. Heavy wastage on both sides, Luftwaffe losing 189 aircraft and Fighter Command 161.

Göring issues orders for next phase. London to be attacked by Kesselring in daylight, and by Sperrle at night, with object of forcing early decision.

Hitler threatens to 'exterminate British cities', and orders 'harassing attacks by day and night', but refuses to sanction indiscriminate bombing of residential districts, claiming that attacks on military objectives are more profitable.

Output of Hurricanes and Spitfires exceeds estimate for August by 69 per cent.

September 7. British Chiefs of Staff learn that moves of barges to Channel ports, concentration of Kesselring's dive-bombers near Straits, and information from captured German agents are thought by experts to point to imminent invasion. Meeting at 5.20 p.m., they sanction bringing of Home Forces to instant readiness.

Between 5 p.m. and 6 p.m. Kesselring attacks London with over 300 bombers and 600 fighters. 21 fighter squadrons engage enemy, mostly after bombing. Heavy damage and casualties in East End dock areas. Luftwaffe lose 41 aircraft in 24 hours, Fighter Command 28.

G.H.Q., Home Forces, call troops to instant readiness by sending 'Invasion imminent' signal at 8.7 p.m.

Sperrle attacks London at night with 250 bombers.

September 9. Kesselring sends 200 bombers to make further daylight attack on London. Park forces half to drop bombs prematurely; edges most of the remainder from primary objectives. Luftwaffe lose 28 aircraft, Fighter Command 19 aircraft and 14 pilots.

September 10. Hitler postpones until 14th decision to give or withhold preliminary order for invasion. Troops to land on 24th if decision favourable.

September 11. Most of 100 bombers sent by Kesselring to make third daylight raid on London reach objectives. Sperrle attacks aircraft factory near Southampton. Luftwaffe lose 29 aircraft, Fighter Command 25.

September 13. Hitler declares at luncheon-table that chances of defeating Britain by air attack are so good that he has no immediate intention of risking hazards of invasion.

Capital ships *Nelson* and *Rodney* join *Hood* at Rosyth. *Repulse*, with aircraft carrier *Furious*, remains at Scapa Flow; *Revenge* at Plymouth. Strong cruiser and destroyer forces already on flanks of invasion area at Portsmouth and Sheerness.

September 14. Hitler tells service chiefs that Göring needs 4 or 5 consecutive fine days to gain air superiority needed for invasion. His decision postponed until 17th. If favourable, troops will land on 27th; otherwise no landing possible before October 8.

Kesselring's fourth daylight raid on London ineffectively opposed. Luftwaffe and Fighter Command each lose 14 aircraft.

September 15. Kesselring throws every available bomber and fighter into two daylight raids on London. Park commits whole force on each occasion, shatters Kesselring's bomber force, and inflicts decisive reverse on his fighter force. Sperrle makes diversionary attacks. Luftwaffe lose 60 aircraft, Fighter Command 26.

Last serious attempt by Luftwaffe to bring Fighter Command to decisive action. Harassing operations continue to supplement night attacks until weather becomes prohibitive.

September 17. Hitler postpones invasion 'until further notice'.

84 barges at Dunkirk sunk or damaged at night by British bombing.

September 18. Hitler sanctions dispersal of invasion fleet to obviate effects of British air and naval action.

September 21. German naval authorities report total of 214 barges lost or damaged out of 1,918 assembled or in transit. Other casualties include 21 transports out of 170.

October 4. Meeting Mussolini at the Brenner, Hitler repeats claim that only lack of 5 consecutive fine days prevented Luftwaffe from gaining air superiority, and blames weather for collapse of his invasion project.

October 12. German Supreme Headquarters formally renounce invasion of Britain in 1940. Revival in spring of 1941 to be considered later.

October 25. 16 Italian bombers, part of contingent sent to Western Front at Mussolini's insistence, make night attack on Harwich. First of series of night attacks by Italian bombers on Harwich, Ipswich, Lowestoft and Yarmouth, continuing until January 2, 1941.

October 29. Italians send 15 bombers and 73 fighters to make daylight attack on objective near North Foreland. No contact with British fighters, but many aircraft hit by anti-aircraft fire.

October 31. Last day of Battle of Britain according to British reckoning.

November 11. 2 Hurricane squadrons intercept 10 Italian bombers and 40 Italian fighters off Harwich. Italian fighter-pilots fight gallantly, but Fiat C.R. 42 is hopelessly outclassed. Italians lose 3 bombers and 3 fighters, Fighter Command no aircraft.

November 23. 29 Italian fighters making offensive sweep meet British fighters off South Foreland and lose 2 aircraft.

November 25. Air Chief Marshal Sir Hugh Dowding succeeded as Air Officer Commanding-in-Chief, Fighter Command, by Air Marshal W. S. Douglas.

Appendix

1 German Higher Organisation and Chain of Command for the Attack on Britain

August 1940

SUPREME COMMAND OF THE ARMED FORCES
Führer and Supreme Commander: Adolf Hitler
Chief of Staff: Field Marshal Keitel
Chief of Operations Staff: General Jodl

ARMY HIGH COMMAND
Commander-in-Chief:
Field-Marshal von Brauchitsch
Chief of General Staff:
General Halder

NAVAL HIGH COMMAND
Commander-in-Chief:
Grand-Admiral Raeder
Chief of Staff:
Admiral Schniewind

LUFTWAFFE HIGH COMMAND
Air Minister and Commander-in-Chief:
Reich Marshal Göring
Chief of General Staff:
General Jeschonnek

ARMY GROUP A
Field-Marshal
von Rundstedt

ARMY GROUP B
Field-Marshal
von Bock

9TH ARMY
General Strauss

16TH ARMY
General Busch

6TH ARMY
Field-Marshal
von Reichenau

LUFTFLOTTE 2
Field-Marshal
Kesselring

LUFTFLOTTE 3
Field-Marshal
Sperrle

LUFTFLOTTE 5
General Stumpff

2 British Higher Organisation and Chain of Command for Home Defence, August 1940

WAR CABINET

Prime Minister and Minister of Defence: W. S. Churchill
Naval, Military and Air Advisors: The Chiefs of Staff

ADMIRALTY
First Lord:
A. V. Alexander
First Sea Lord:
Admiral Sir Dudley
Pound

WAR OFFICE
Secretary of State:
A. Eden
*Chief of the Imperial
General Staff:*
Field-Marshal Sir J. Dill

AIR MINISTRY
Secretary of State:
Sir A. Sinclair
Chief of Air Staff:
Air Chief Marshal Sir C. Newall

HOME FLEET
Admiral of the Fleet
Sir C. Forbes

ROSYTH COMMAND
Vice-Admiral
C. G. Ramsay

NORE COMMAND
Admiral The Hon. Sir R.
Plunkett-Ernle-Erle-Drax

DOVER COMMAND
Vice- Admiral
Sir B. Ramsay

**PORTSMOUTH
COMMAND**
Admiral Sir W. James

**WESTERN
APPROACHES
COMMAND**
Admiral Sir M.
Dunbar-Nasmith, V.C.

HOME FORCES
Commander-in-Chief:
General Sir A. Brooke
Chief of General Staff:
Lieutenant-General
B. Paget

**SCOTTISH
COMMAND**

**NORTHERN
COMMAND**

**EASTERN
COMMAND**

**SOUTHERN
COMMAND**

**WESTERN
COMMAND**

AA COMMAND
Lieutenant-
General Sir
F. Pile, Bt.

FIGHTER COMMAND
Air Chief Marshal
Sir H. Dowding

BALLOON COMMAND
Air Vice-Marshal O. T. Boyd

OBSERVER CORPS
Air Commodore A. D.
Warrington-Morris

No. 10 GROUP
Air Vice-Marshal Sir Q. Brand

No. 11 GROUP
Air Vice-Marshal K. R. Park

No. 12 GROUP
Air Vice-Marshal
T. L. Leigh-Mallory

No. 13 GROUP
Air Vice-Marshal R. E. Saul

**BOMBER
COMMAND**
Air Marshal
Sir C. Portal

**BOMBER
GROUPS**

**COASTAL
COMMAND**
Air Marshal
Sir F. Bowhill

**COASTAL
GROUPS**

Short Bibliography

ASHMORE, Major-General E. B., *Air Defence*, 1929
BISHOP, Edward, *The Battle of Britain*, 1960
O'BRIEN, T. H., *Civil Defence*, 1955
BUTLER, Sir James, *Grand Strategy, Vol. II*, 1957
CHURCHILL, Sir Winston S., *Their Finest Hour*, 1949
COLLIER, Basil, *The Defence of the United Kingdom*, 1957
  Leader of the Few, 1957
DEERE, Group-Captain Alan C., *Nine Lives*, 1959
FLEMING, Peter, *Invasion 1940*, 1957
GALLAND, Adolf, *The First and the Last*, 1955
GRINNELL-MILNE, Duncan, *The Silent Victory*, 1958
HITLER, Adolf, *Mein Kampf (My Struggle)*, English Edition, 1939
JOHNSON, Group-Captain J. E., *Wing Leader*, 1956
KESSELRING, Field-Marshal, *The Memoirs of Field-Marshal Kesselring*, 1954
MCKEE, Alexander, *Strike from the Sky*, 1960
MANSTEIN, Field-Marshal Erich von, *Lost Victories*, 1958
MARTIENSSEN, Anthony, *Hitler and His Admirals*, 1948
MIDDLETON, Drew, *The Sky Suspended*, 1960
MUGGERIDGE, Malcolm (Editor), *Ciano's Diary, 1939–43*, 1947
  Ciano's Diplomatic Papers, 1948
PILE, General Sir Frederick, *Ack-Ack*, 1947
RICHARDS, Denis, *The Fight at Odds*, 1953
SHULMAN, Milton, *Defeat in the West*, 1947
WALLACE, Graham, *R.A.F. Biggin Hill*, 1957
WHEATLEY, Ronald, *Operation Sea Lion*, 1958
WILMOT, Chester, *The Struggle for Europe*, 1952
WOOD, Derek, and DEMPSTER, Derek, *The Narrow Margin*, 1961
WYKEHAM, Peter, *Fighter Command*, 1960

Index

The numerals in **bold** type refer to the *figure* number of the illustrations

Pownall, Lieutenant-General H. R., 164

Purfleet, fires at, after the first September raid on London, **38**

Radar chain brought into operation, 163
early warning system, 19, Chap. 3 and *passim*
station, 300-foot mast of a, **11**

R.D.F. (Radio Direction Finding), *see* Radar

Raeder, Grand-Admiral, 30, 32, 35–38, 124, 154, 164, 165; **4, 5**

Ramsay, Vice-Admiral Sir Bertram, 70, **173**

Ramsay, Vice-Admiral C. G., 173

Reichenau, Field-Marshal von, 38

Repulse, 170

Revenge, 170

Reynaud, M., French Premier, 164

Richthofen Geschwader, 36

Rochester, aircraft factory at, 90, 105

Rochford, 105, 108

Rodney, capital ship, 170

Rome-Berlin Axis, 159

Royal Aeroplane Factory at Farnborough, 78

Royal Aircraft Establishment, Farnborough, 78

Rudloe aerodrome, 83, 141

Runstedt, Field-Marshal von, 30, 172

Russia, Germany signs pact with, 163

Saint-Cloud, Sperrle's headquarters at, 59

Saul, Air Vice-Marshal R. E., 25, 86–89; **21**

Scandinavian campaign, 20

Scapa Flow, raids on, 63, 76

Seaham harbour, 88

Sealand maintenance unit at, 109

Sector Station, operations room of a, **12**

Sèvres, German air corps headquarters at, 59

Shanghai attacked by Japanese (1932, 159)

Sheerness, 78, 80

Sheppey, Isle of, 79

Short aircraft factory, 90

Silvertown, 130

Simon, Sir John, 161

Six, Professor Dr., 37

Sixth Army (German), 38

Sixteenth Army (German), 38

Somme, Battle of the, 66, 88, 110

South-coast beach, summer 1940, **37**

South Shields, air attack on, 105

Southampton, aircraft factory near, 138
attack on, 84, 170

Spanish Civil War, 19

Sperrle, Field-Marshal Hugo, 20, 25, 29, 59–61, 63, 71–77, 80, 83–85, 87, 94–96, 98, 100, 105, 107, 109, 122, 124, 134, 141, 152, 153, 155, 165–169; **9**

Spitfire aircraft, 39, 40, 63, 70, 79, 80, 84–86, 88, 90, 93, 94, 97, 99, 103, 119, 125, 141, 142, 149, 150, 155, 161, 163–167, 169; **24, 46**

Sportspalast, Hitler's speech at, 123

Squadrons (Fighter Command):
No. 1, 108
No. 19, 118
No. 46, 89n.
No. 54, 70, 99, 118
No. 56, 64, 105, 119, 121
No. 72, 87, 142
No. 74, 80
No. 92, 142